COOK

COCKTAILS
CUISINE
CULTURE

BY

VIE®

PUBLISHED BY

@2023 Cornerstone Marketing and Advertising, Inc. — The Idea Boutique®
All rights reserved.

114 Logan Lane, Suite 4, Grayton Beach, FL 32459
E-mail: Info@TheIdeaBoutique.com

Creative Director: Lisa Burwell

Production Manager: Gerald F. Burwell

Author/Editor: Jordan Staggs

Graphic Designers: Tracey Thomas, Hannah Vermillion

Chief Copy Editor: Margaret Stevenson

Library of Congress Control Number: 2023946093

ISBN-13: 978-0-9989149-6-1

Printed in Canada

Great food, drinks, and experiences are nourishing for the soul. We dedicate this book, the follow-up to *HOME—Inspirations for Home and Life by VIE*, to all the incredible chefs, restaurateurs, mixologists, service staff, and creatives who foster glorious dining experiences throughout our beautiful area along the Gulf Coast of Northwest Florida.

We also dedicate it to members of our culinary community who were recently lost but will never be forgotten:

To the late Harriet Crommelin, founder and owner of the iconic Café Thirty-A in Seagrove Beach, thank you for your unlimited kindness and the generosity you showed not only to all those who entered your establishment but also to our area nonprofits serving others in need. Your friendship and support of *VIE* mean the world to us.

To Chef Mark Anton (Borago Restaurant, Grayton Beach) and Chef Brannon Janca (Stinky's Fish Camp and Down Island Gulf Seafood Restaurant, Santa Rosa Beach), thank you for sharing your gifts with us and treating every customer like family.

You are all missed, but your legacy and hospitality will endure through this community.

—Lisa and Gerald Burwell and the *VIE* Team

Great Southern Café

COOK by *VIE*

Cocktails. Cuisine. Culture.

Since *VIE* magazine's inception, its mission has been to tell rich, vibrant human-interest "Stories with Heart and Soul" about the people, places, and happenings in a region coined "COLA 2 COLA®" by the publication's creators. Florida's coastal communities from Pensacola to Apalachicola are near and dear to the hearts of *VIE*'s publishers and audience. There seems to be an inherently creative and talented pool of people drawn to this beachside haven. People flock to the Gulf of Mexico and adjacent bright white sands to be inspired and inspire others, just as *VIE*'s makers have. Cofounders Lisa and Gerald Burwell and the pioneers of *VIE*'s early days recognized this pool of talent and authentic creativity and the need to share stories with the world about the slice of heaven they called home.

Fast-forward to 2020, when *VIE* released its first luxury coffee-table book, *HOME: Inspirations for Home and Life by VIE*. This photographic tome celebrates stories of talented architects, builders, and interior designers throughout the COLA 2 COLA region, and there are many! The book also includes "pause pages" throughout, featuring local landmarks, events, past *VIE* highlights, and restaurants.

The latter is what inspired this book. *COOK: Cocktails. Cuisine. Culture.* is a love letter to the incredible world-class chefs, restaurateurs, event planners, and culinary teams who bring the zest of life to this region—the place we residents call home and millions of others call their home away from home each year. From the old favorite restaurants that locals and vacationers visit time and again to the new eateries on the block, we can't deny that the dining and cocktail scene in the area—particularly that twenty-or-so-mile stretch in Walton County, including Miramar Beach and the affluent Scenic Highway 30-A— is unforgettable.

We welcome you to join our table as we sip, savor, and celebrate on a culinary tour of this coastal paradise.

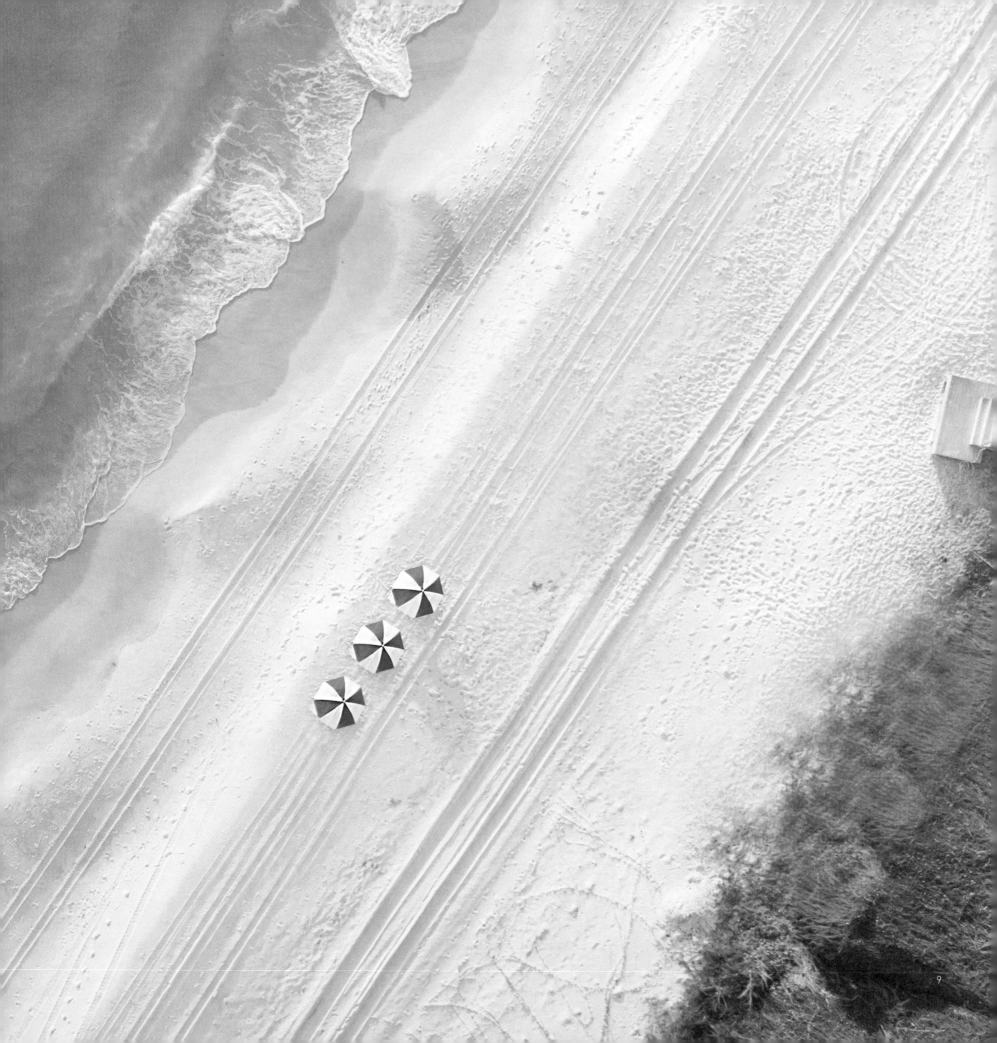

Sandestin

A true resort town boasting numerous destinations from the beach to the bay, Sandestin Golf and Beach Resort comprises multiple communities, properties, and entertainment hubs in Miramar Beach, Florida. These include Grand Boulevard Town Center, Hilton Sandestin Beach Golf Resort and Spa, The Market Shops, the Village of Baytowne Wharf, and more. Relax, eat, shop, and explore!

Vin'tij Food & Wine

A Culinary Legend and His Legacy

Emeril Lagasse *on* Food, Family, *and* Giving Back

"On March 26, 1990, I opened the doors of my flagship restaurant, Emeril's," says renowned celebrity chef Emeril Lagasse, whose award-winning cuisine and energetic network television cooking shows have gained him international recognition since the early 1990s. "Over the past thirty-three years, I've had the opportunity and pleasure to embrace the city of New Orleans and work toward being the best restaurant for New Orleanians." Since then, he has also opened several other restaurants, including those still operating today: Emeril's and Meril in New Orleans, Delmonico Steakhouse and Emeril's New Orleans Fish House in Las Vegas, and Emeril's Coastal in Miramar Beach, Florida.

It's Miramar Beach and the surrounding area where we find Emeril spending much of his (minimal) free time, as he and his wife, Alden, moved to nearby Santa Rosa Beach around the turn of the millennium. Alden's family ties to the area drew them in, as did the gorgeous white-sand beaches and incredible recreation opportunities, from sportfishing to golf. It also turned out to be the perfect place to raise their youngest children, E.J. and Meril. The Lagasses are known for generously giving back to the community through working with local nonprofits such as Food For Thought and the Seaside Neighborhood School.

Emeril and Alden also give back to New Orleans programs and other national organizations through the Emeril Lagasse Foundation, founded in 2002 with a mission "to create opportunities to inspire, mentor, and enable youth to reach their full potential through culinary, nutrition, and arts education with a focus on life skills development." November marked the twentieth anniversary of the foundation's Carnivale du Vin weekend in New Orleans, one of its three annual signature fund-raisers.

Shortly after the foundation's twentieth anniversary, E.J. Lagasse also turned twenty, and he is already carving a name for himself in the culinary world alongside his father. At the age of thirteen, he began working in the kitchen at Emeril's Coastal. Concerning Emeril's Coastal, Emeril says he was shooting episodes of his Amazon series *Eat the World with Emeril Lagasse* along Italy's Amalfi Coast when he realized how similar its fishing communities and culture were to the beach communities in Northwest Florida. He was inspired to open Emeril's Coastal, whose modern take on fresh seafood, craft cocktails, and decadent desserts has drawn customers to the Grand Boulevard Town Center since it opened in 2017. Although the menu has undergone some refreshes since then, fresh-off-the-boat seafood is still front and center.

Emeril and E.J. Lagasse
at Emeril's Restaurant
in New Orleans

E.J., too, has evolved from a bright-eyed kid learning the ropes into a powerhouse leading man. When E.J. was fifteen and working in the kitchen at Emeril's Coastal, Emeril told *VIE*, "I tell him to be serious about it and just keep learning something new every day." In addition to his father—whom he also refers to as his best friend—E.J. counts chefs Éric Ripert, José Andrés, Daniel Boulud, and Frank Szymanski among his mentors. He graduated from Johnson & Wales University (his dad's alma mater) and is now the chef patron at Emeril's flagship restaurant in New Orleans.

"Since 1990, Emeril's cuisine has been inspired by Louisiana heritage and has evolved through cultural and generational influences," says Emeril, calling the current menu a refined and elegant approach to Louisiana cooking. "Now, more than ever, I am excited for the future of Emeril's and proud that my son, E.J., has joined me as chef patron and taken the reins in the kitchen. E.J. is a risk-taker, and his passion for refinement is contagious. We have exciting things planned and are committed to improving our craft one dish, one experience, and one renovation at a time."

Emeril's restaurant "has undergone a huge transition, and we are gearing up for a renovation in July," says the elder Lagasse. Guests in the main dining room will choose from a classic or seasonal tasting menu, while à la carte dining is available in the salon.

Emeril's

"I cherish every moment we get to spend in this building with our team and our guests," says E.J. of Emeril's restaurant. "I grew up in this restaurant and cannot wait to share the many exciting things coming soon." This father-son partnership is the beginning of what's sure to be a family legacy, with the torch passing to E.J. on many restaurant projects in the future as Emeril continues building his brand and supporting the foundation's many efforts.

In addition, Emeril's Table in the Louis Armstrong New Orleans International Airport was honored as the best local-inspired airport restaurant at the AX Awards in 2023. Emeril also hosts the streaming series *Emeril Cooks* and *Emeril Tailgates* on Roku and sells his name-brand cookware and kitchen tools via HSN. And, as if there wasn't already enough on his plate, the celeb chef was recently named the first-ever chief culinary officer for Carnival Cruise Lines, where he'll "be bringing his eye for excitement and his legendary taste for flavor to all onboard restaurants."

Through every menu, fund-raiser, restaurant, television series, and project, Emeril insists it takes a village to achieve success. "I am grateful for my team, whom I learn from daily, the restaurants' loyal guests, and our community," he says. "As the journey continues, I am incredibly humbled and thankful for everyone who has been part of it with us."

Emeril, Alden, and E.J. Lagasse at The Heritage – A *VIE* Legacy Show Home reveal party in Seagrove Beach

E.J.'s salmon cheesecake
at Emeril's Restaurant

Brandy Milk Punch

By Emeril's

Ingredients

- 2 ounces E&J Vanilla Brandy
- ½ ounce rich simple syrup
- 2 ounces whole milk
- Ground nutmeg, for garnish

Directions

Shake all ingredients in a cocktail shaker, strain
into a brandy or wine glass over fresh ice, and top
with a dusting of ground nutmeg.

Shrimp & Andouille Gumbo

By Emeril's

A NEW ORLEANS FAVORITE FROM THE MASTER CHEF HIMSELF!

Ingredients

- 1 quart roux (directions follow)
- 1 pound okra, chopped
- 1 pound andouille sausage, chopped
- 1 pound yellow onion, diced
- ¾ pound green bell pepper, diced
- ¾ pound celery, chopped
- 1 clove garlic, minced
- 2 bay leaves
- ½ teaspoon dried thyme
- ½ teaspoon dried oregano
- ¼ teaspoon dried cayenne pepper
- ½ tablespoon Emeril's Essence
- ½ teaspoon black pepper
- 2 pounds medium shrimp, peeled and deveined
- 4 quarts shrimp stock
- ½ tablespoon Crystal Hot Sauce
- ½ tablespoon Lea & Perrins Worcestershire Sauce

Directions

MAKE A DARK ROUX:

Heat 1 cup oil in a large soup pot over high heat. When oil begins to smoke, whisk in 1 ½ cups flour. Continue to whisk constantly until the mixture is a rich brown color. Be careful not to produce specs of black. Roux must remain an even color throughout the process. If specks appear, you must start over. When the roux is mahogany-colored, add onions, celery, and bell pepper.

Stir the mixture until the vegetables are softened. Add okra and garlic and cook for 1 minute. Slowly whisk in the stock along with the Worcestershire, hot sauce, and cayenne. Season lightly with salt and pepper and bring the liquid to a boil. Add bay leaves, oregano, and thyme, and simmer until the flavors begin to come together, about 45 minutes.

Add the sausage and continue to cook until the gumbo reaches the desired thickness and is rich and flavorful, about 1 hour longer.

Stir in the shrimp and green onions. Taste and adjust seasonings, if necessary. Cook until the shrimp are cooked through and the onions have softened, 15 to 20 minutes longer. Serve with rice. *Bon appétit!*

Emeril's

Charcuterie and small
bites created by Emeril
and his team for The
Heritage – A *VIE* Legacy
Show Home reveal party

"

Eating well gives a spectacular joy to life and contributes immensely to goodwill and happy companionship.

—ELSA SCHIAPARELLI

Island-inspired cuisine
and cocktails at Daytrader
Tiki Bar & Restaurant

Dreams Do Come True
A Culinary Family Legacy

Many children have big dreams of being professional actors or astronauts, though very few turn those early-age career aspirations into reality. Jack McGuckin knew from childhood that he wanted to be a chef. His heroes were the likes of Julia Child and Jacques Pépin instead of Neil Armstrong. Now he co-owns and operates Bijoux, a casual fine-dining experience located in The Market Shops in Miramar Beach, Florida, alongside his wife, Leslie, who purchased the restaurant in 2008. The menu is a blend of fresh Gulf seafood and globally inspired specialty dishes. Bijoux also offers an extensive wine list and craft cocktails in the sumptuous bar and lounge.

Leslie remains integral to Bijoux's operations and is a world-class floral and interior designer who keeps the restaurant looking beautiful. Together, she and Jack provide memorable dining experiences for patrons daily in a chic, contemporary atmosphere that evokes the Big Easy more than the beach. Indeed, French and Creole dishes, such as crab beignets, shrimp remoulade, grouper almondine, and crème brûlée, are hallmarks of the restaurant's "coastal cuisine with New Orleans flair." Bijoux has been awarded *Florida Trend*'s Golden Spoon Award annually since 2017 and has received many other accolades, including numerous *Wine Spectator* Awards

of Excellence, Diners' Choice by OpenTable, and Tripadvisor Travelers' Choice Awards.

Making a difference in the community is also essential to Jack and Leslie, who work with numerous local nonprofits through wine dinner fund-raisers—both in the restaurant and at private homes—and other special events. Their desire to give back to the area that received Bijoux with open arms also sets a fine example for their children, who say they want to carry on the family tradition when they're older. "Our son wants to be the chef one day, and our daughter wants to own the restaurant and be able to eat Nutella ice cream whenever she pleases," Leslie says.

The family extends to Bijoux's staff, as well, and many have worked there for years. With team members having hailed from the Gulf Coast, Thailand, Brazil, Eastern Europe, Jamaica, Ukraine, Kazakhstan, and more, the restaurant's menu often reflects the diversity in cultures and flavors. Chef McGuckin sees each new team member's culinary traditions as a learning experience and is inspired by his travels. Incorporating different world cuisines and techniques into the menu creates a one-of-a-kind experience for diners, whether they have visited Bijoux once or one hundred times.

Chef Jack McGuckin

Bijoux

Royal Red Shrimp Remoulade

By Bijoux

Ingredients

FOR THE BOIL

- 1 pound Royal Red shrimp
- 6 quarts water
- 2 teaspoons liquid crab boil
- 1 yellow onion, diced
- 4 stalks celery, diced
- 3 lemons, quartered
- 1 cup white wine
- 3 tablespoons kosher salt
- 2 bay leaves
- 1 tablespoon black peppercorns
- 1 cinnamon stick
- 2 quarts of ice

FOR THE REMOULADE

- 1 jalapeño, seeded and roasted
- 1 cup (1 bunch) Italian parsley, chopped
- ¼ teaspoon ground black pepper
- ½ tablespoon kosher salt
- ½ teaspoon minced garlic
- ¼ small red onion, minced
- 2 tablespoons capers
- 2 tablespoons creole mustard
- 1 ¼ cup mayonnaise
- 1 tablespoon lemon juice

FOR THE PICKLED MUSTARD SEED

- 1 cup yellow mustard seed
- 1 ½ cups water
- 1 ½ cups rice wine vinegar
- ½ cup sugar
- 1 tablespoon kosher salt

FOR THE FENNEL SALAD

- 1 bulb fennel, stalk removed and reserved, bulb halved and sliced very thin on a mandoline
- ½ of the fennel fronds from the same bulb, ripped into smaller pieces
- 2 tablespoons extra-virgin olive oil
- Juice of ½ lemon
- Salt and pepper to taste

Directions

FOR THE BOIL:

In a large pot, bring all ingredients except shrimp and ice to a boil, then turn down to a simmer for 20 minutes. Turn back to a rapid boil and add shrimp. Stir to make sure the shrimp are submerged. Once the water begins to bubble again, turn off the heat and let sit for 3 minutes. Move the pot to a sink and add the ice to the pot to stop the shrimp cooking. After 5 minutes, pull the shrimp from the ice, peel, and devein.

FOR THE REMOULADE:

Add all ingredients except the mayonnaise, mustard, and lemon juice to a food processor and blend well, stopping and scraping down the sides of the processor as needed. Add the remaining ingredients and mix to combine.

FOR THE PICKLED MUSTARD SEED:

Combine all ingredients in a saucepan and bring to a simmer for 45 minutes, stirring occasionally.

TO ASSEMBLE THE DISH:

Toss half a dozen boiled shrimp in the remoulade and mix to coat the shrimp completely. Arrange some of the fennel salad in the bottom of a martini glass and top with the shrimp. Add a spoonful of the pickled mustard seed and some fennel fronds to garnish. Enjoy!

Bouillabaisse

By Bijoux

Ingredients

FOR THE BOUILLABAISSE

- ½ cup extra-virgin olive oil
- 1 cup chopped onion
- 1 cup chopped fennel
- 4 cloves garlic, smashed
- 2 or 3 large, ripe tomatoes, chopped (or 2 cups canned)
- 2 ½ quarts water
- Fresh herb sprigs: thyme, parsley, fennel fronds, and basil
- ½ teaspoon saffron threads
- 2 tablespoons sea salt
- 3–4 pounds fish heads, bones, trimmings, and shrimp shells
- 2 lobster tails, shells removed
- 1 pound peeled shrimp (save the shells for the stock)
- 1 pound grouper, snapper, or other flaky white fish, cut into large chunks
- ½ pound jumbo lump crab, picked to remove shells
- 12 Gulf oysters, shucked (reserve liquid)
- 1 pound mussels or clams, scrubbed and mussels debearded
- 3 tablespoons butter
- 1 cup cooked Israeli couscous
- ½ cup chiffonade basil
- Crusty bread, sliced, brushed with extra-virgin olive oil, and toasted

FOR THE ROUILLE

- 1 teaspoon chili paste
- 1 teaspoon lemon juice
- ½ teaspoon minced garlic
- 1 small pinch saffron threads
- 2 cups mayonnaise

Directions

FOR THE ROUILLE:

Mix all ingredients to combine.

FOR THE BOUILLABAISSE:

Heat the oil in a tall pot over medium heat. Add the onion and chopped fennel and cook gently until softened. Stir in the garlic and cook for a minute until fragrant, then add the tomatoes, water, herbs, saffron, salt, and fish bones and shrimp shells. Bring to a simmer, then reduce heat so that the broth bubbles slowly without boiling.

Cook for 30 minutes, then strain the broth into a large bowl or another pot and discard the solids.

Pour the broth back into the stockpot and bring to a boil. Add the lobster and clams or mussels, and cook for two minutes. Add the fish and shellfish, cover, and simmer until the mussels or clams open (this will only take a few minutes). Stir in the crab and oysters, cover, and cook for two more minutes.

Add the butter and couscous and stir over low heat until the butter is melted and the couscous is hot. Taste the soup and add more salt and freshly ground pepper if needed. Finally, add the basil. Portion seafood and broth equally among bowls. Top with crusty grilled bread smeared with rouille. Bon appétit!

Pear Lychee Martini

By Bijoux

Ingredients

FOR THE LYCHEE SIMPLE SYRUP

- 6 lychees, peeled
- 1 cup granulated sugar
- 1 cup water

FOR THE COCKTAIL

- 2 ounces pear vodka
- 1 ounce sparkling wine
- ½ ounce lychee liqueur
- ¼ ounce lychee simple syrup (directions follow)
- ¼ ounce freshly squeezed lemon juice
- Dehydrated lemon slice, for garnish

Directions

FOR THE LYCHEE SIMPLE SYRUP:

Muddle or smash lychees and set to the side. Add the water and sugar to a saucepan. Bring to a simmer over medium heat. Add in the lychees and stir, pressing lightly on the fruit. Let the syrup reduce and thicken, then take it off the heat. Let the syrup cool. Once cooled, place the syrup in the fridge for 1 hour to let the flavor from the lychees permeate the syrup. Pour the lychee syrup through a sieve to strain.

FOR THE COCKTAIL:

In a cocktail shaker, add pear vodka, lychee liqueur, lychee simple syrup, and lemon juice. Add ice. Shake well and strain into a cold martini glass. Top with sparkling wine. Set the dehydrated lemon slice right on top to finish. Sip and enjoy!

> **"**
>
> I'm a little old school, a little classic New American cuisine; E.J. reads my books from cover to cover to make sure he's doing things correctly, but he has unbelievable training and vision.

—CHEF EMERIL LAGASSE, *VIE* SPEAKS PODCAST

Primed and Ready
Northwest Florida's Four-Star Gem

In the Gulf-front Hilton Sandestin Beach Golf Resort & Spa, a hidden gem awaits those who venture down the grand stairway and through the rich wooden doors to the area's only AAA Four-Diamond steakhouse. With the finest aged USDA prime steaks, fresh seafood from the Gulf Coast and around the globe, a six-hundred-label wine list, and a rotating craft cocktail menu, Seagar's Prime Steaks & Seafood has something for everyone. The New York–style dining experience has long been heralded as one of the best around. In recent years, the Hilton and Seagar's team have taken things up several notches and have big plans for the future—as in, Michelin-star big.

"Now that our patrons have grown to trust our culinary boldness outside of the tried-and-true staples of Seagar's, it allows us to create dishes that press into the avant-garde," says executive chef Fleetwood Covington III, who designs each seasonal menu to include creative new dishes and new spins on some familiar favorites. "It makes us better to constantly push boundaries, and I always write the next menu with that in mind."

Some things one might find on those menus, for example, could range from Alaskan king crab cakes and the freshest Gulf grouper to tender Japanese A5 wagyu beef and flavorful red stag venison. Specials might include handmade pasta, such as a floral-printed cannelloni with beet beurre blanc. Exquisite plating and unique dishware add another layer to the dining experience. The details make each seasonal menu worth returning to try, as no two dinners will be the same.

The twenty-seat bar and adjacent lounge offer a luxurious ambience for patrons awaiting their table or those who stop by for after-work drinks, with live piano music setting the scene and a sophisticated vibe reminiscent of the metropolitan steakhouses that inspired the restaurant. Private dining in the Seagar's wine rooms is available for groups, special occasions, corporate events, and more—but the best seats are in the main dining room, where diners can see all the action happening in the open-air concept kitchen led by Covington.

Seagar's is also a popular venue for charity events; the restaurant partners with many area nonprofits that give back to the community, including Sinfonia Gulf Coast, Habitat for Humanity, Destin Charity Wine Auction Foundation, Children's Volunteer Health Network, Emerald Coast Autism Center, Emerald Coast Children's Advocacy Center, Sandcastle Kids, and more.

39

Seared Copper River Salmon

By Chef Fleetwood Covington III, Seagar's

SERVES 4

Ingredients

- 28 ounces Copper River salmon
- 2 pounds beets, peeled
- 16 ounces morel mushrooms
- 16 ounces fiddlehead ferns
- 1 pound butter
- 3 shallots, peeled
- 3 ounces garlic
- 4 stalks white asparagus
- 1 container of mustard blossoms
- 1 package of Boursin herbed garlic cheese
- Blended oil (75% canola, 25% extra-virgin olive oil)
- White cooking wine

Directions

Evenly portion salmon into 7-ounce fillets, ensuring all bones have been removed. Season the skin with salt and pepper and set aside.

Slice white asparagus into ¼-inch rounds and set aside. Rinse morel mushrooms to remove any dirt from foraging and set aside. Rinse fiddlehead ferns of any debris and set aside.

Peel beets and roast for 45 minutes or until soft. In a blender, puree beets with the Boursin, salt, pepper, and a teaspoon of white wine, and set aside.

Preheat oven to 400°F. Pour 2 tablespoons of blended oil into a pan on high and place salmon fillets skin-side down for 1 minute or until skin is thoroughly seared. Flip the fillets, add a splash of white wine, add butter, and then place the pan in the oven for 5 to 6 minutes.

In a separate sauté pan, add butter and combine asparagus, fiddlehead ferns, and morels and gently sauté with shallots. Deglaze with a splash of white wine as needed. Once the veggies are cooked, assemble them on your plates.

Remove the fish from the oven and arrange on top of the vegetable mix.

Combine the beet puree with unsalted butter in a blender until a bright pink color forms, and pour symmetrically on a blank space on the plate.

To garnish, add mustard blossoms atop the beet reduction. Serve and enjoy!

Fit for a Queen

By Seagar's

Ingredients

- 1 ounce Beefeater Pink Strawberry Gin
- ½ ounce St-Germain Elderflower Liqueur
- 3 ounces brut rosé Champagne
- Candied hibiscus flower, for garnish

Directions

Shake gin and St-Germain with ice and strain into a coupe glass. Top with brut rosé Champagne, and garnish with candied hibiscus flower. Cheers!

"

Dessert is a necessity of life.

—ADRIENNE POSEY

Grape Expectations
Fine Wine, Food, *and* Family

Culinary delights are served daily at Vin'tij Food & Wine, a Northwest Florida favorite along the Gulf Coast in Miramar Beach. What started as a wine market and casual fine-dining café in 1998 has evolved into an all-day hot spot in the bustling Grand Boulevard Town Center, where it moved in 2018 and started a new chapter. Owners Todd and Sabrina Reber aim to create unique culinary experiences for all their customers, whether stopping in for lunch with the girls, a business meeting, a "Wine Down" happy hour, or an upscale dinner with family and friends. Congratulations to this local institution on twenty-five years in business!

The Vin'tij patio offers alfresco dining amid the lively town center. Inside, visitors will find a fully stocked wine market, an expansive bar, and a comfortable yet elegant dining room outfitted in rich coastal blues and rustic wood accents. A private room is a perfect spot for guests' special occasions, visiting winemaker dinners, community fund-raisers, and more. Meanwhile, a mosaic tree along one wall represents the "Reber family tree," as Sabrina has called it; she and Todd worked on the piece together with their two children, and the name Reber aptly means "keeper of the vine."

The keepers are living up to that legacy by offering guests a robust menu with longtime favorites and rotating seasonal, nature-inspired items curated by partnering chef Ignacio Bernal. Todd Reber describes Bernal as the "creative inspiration for the majority of our menus, special events, and four-course wine dinners." In addition, chef Jimbo Butler, who has been with Vin'tij for around twenty years, oversees the integrity of the original recipes that are so loved by regulars.

The kitchen and front-of-house teams know that customers expect casual excellence when they visit Vin'tij, whether on vacation or for a weekly locals' lunch. Fine wine is always on hand, as are fresh fruit mimosas at brunch, and for those who feel adventurous, daily specials ensure the chance to try something new. Rest assured—many guests return for their must-have staples, including the pecan chicken, the oyster BLT, the shrimp and grits, and Chef Bernal's daily fish presentation.

This dedication to the customer experience has predictably garnered many awards for Vin'tij and its team, including multiple *Florida Trend* Golden Spoon Awards and recognitions from the Best of the Emerald Coast, Tripadvisor, and Restaurant Guru.

And remember to save room for dessert! From the crowd-favorite warm griddled lemon pound cake to Sabrina's vegan and gluten-free delights and more, the last course of any meal at Vin'tij is sure to be mouthwatering.

Lobster Pasta

with Champagne Vanilla Black Pepper Cream

By Vin'tij

SERVES 2

Ingredients

- 2 lobster tails, 6 ounces each
- 4 ounces unsalted butter, melted
- 6 ounces rock shrimp
- 2 tablespoons olive oil
- 8 ounces cooked linguine (boiled and drained)
- 1 teaspoon vanilla paste
- 6 ounces brut Champagne
- 8 ounces heavy cream
- 2 tablespoons shallots, finely diced
- 2 tablespoons red bell pepper, finely diced
- 2 tablespoons yellow bell pepper, finely diced
- 1 tablespoon garlic, minced
- 1 teaspoon fresh cracked black pepper
- 1 teaspoon kosher salt
- Additional salt and pepper for seasoning lobster and rock shrimp
- Cooking oil for fryer

Directions

Turn the oven on broil. Cut the tops of the lobster lengthwise and pull the meat apart from the shell. Place the lobster back in its shell. Coat the lobster with 4 ounces of butter and season with salt and pepper. Broil the lobster tails until lightly browned, about 5 to 10 minutes. Remove them from the oven and set aside but keep warm.

In a fryer, heat oil to 350°F. Once the oil is hot, carefully place cooked linguine in the pot and fry until golden brown. Remove with a slotted spoon and place on a plate with a paper towel to drain.

In a pan, sauté rock shrimp in olive oil on medium heat for 30 seconds. Sprinkle it with salt and pepper. Remove the shrimp and set aside. To the pan, add the shallots, garlic, and red and yellow peppers. Cook for an additional minute. Deglaze the pan with Champagne. Add heavy cream and vanilla paste. Reduce sauce by a fourth. Add the shrimp back to the pan and season with the kosher salt and cracked black pepper. Turn off the heat but keep warm.

Place crispy pasta onto the plates. Spread the broiled lobster tail throughout the pasta. Drizzle the pan sauce and shrimp over the pasta and lobster. Bon appétit!

Beet Salad

By Vin'tij

SERVES 2

Ingredients

- 3 baby red beets, roasted and peeled
- 3 baby yellow beets, roasted and peeled

FOR THE WHIPPED CITRUS GOAT CHEESE

- 1 cup goat cheese
- 2 oranges, zested and juiced
- 2 lemons, zested and juiced
- 2 limes, zested and juiced
- 1 teaspoon honey

FOR GARNISH

- Baby arugula
- Fresh raspberries
- Purple orchid petals
- Toasted walnuts
- Olive oil
- Balsamic reduction
- Salt and pepper

Directions

Cut roasted beets into small cubes. Set aside.

Place goat cheese, honey, citrus juices, and zest in a food processor and blend.

With a spoon, spread ½ cup of the goat cheese onto the plates.

Place the beets on the plate and alternate raspberries, arugula, and orchid petals in between the beets. Sprinkle the plate with toasted walnuts, salt, and pepper. Drizzle the salad with olive oil and balsamic reduction.

Strawberry Raspberry Mimosa

By Vin'tij

YIELDS 6 CUPS

Ingredients

- 1 cup water
- 1 cup sugar
- 2 cups fresh strawberries
- 2 cups fresh raspberries
- ⅓ cup lemon juice
- Champagne or Prosecco (optional)

Directions

Place water and sugar in a pot and bring to a boil to dissolve the sugar.

Place the berries in a blender and add dissolved sugar water. Blend well.

Place in a fine sieve or in a nut milk bag to strain and remove seeds.

Add lemon juice to the puree and mix. Place in the refrigerator for up to 5 days. Add juice to your favorite Champagne or Prosecco for a spirited morning mimosa. Cheers!

Rose & Co.

Floral Inspirations

Table settings, events, and special occasions seem incomplete without beautiful blooms, but Rose & Co. Flowers in Grand Boulevard Town Center can provide for all of those situations and more. The charming lifestyle boutique-meets-floral design studio is resplendent with flowers, home decor, candles and fragrances, designer tableware, books, jewelry, gifts, and much more. The one-stop shop indeed holds something to please everyone, whether you're shopping for Mother's Day, a birthday, or something special to let loved ones know they are appreciated.

Owner and principal designer Cari DeGregorio has an extensive background in event and floral design and has brought her prowess into this venture, which she opened in 2021. The European-inspired shop will make visitors feel like they've stumbled upon a secret garden or a hidden retail gem mixing antique, rustic, and contemporary design. The full-service florist is ready to please with the most beautiful petals to create an arrangement for any occasion, with pickup and delivery options available.

Every day deserves beautiful blooms!

30A

If you are a resident of southern Walton County in Florida, you've probably been asked, "What is 30A?" The technical answer is that it's a nickname for Scenic Highway 30-A, the eighteen-mile coastal route that runs parallel to the Gulf of Mexico between Miramar Beach and Panama City Beach. It bisects a collection of unique beach communities, holding some of the best restaurants, architecture, art, and cultural events in the US. The short answer: 30A is a way of life.

Forging a Culinary Empire
From Pensacola *to* 30A

Chef Jim Shirley's repertoire is certainly not lacking in diversity. His restaurants range from the well-known Great Southern Café in Seaside, Florida—fittingly serving Southern favorites for breakfast, lunch, and dinner—to Farm & Fire, North Beach Social, The C-Bar, The Chicken Shack, and even The Meltdown on 30A, which offers gourmet grilled-cheese sandwiches from a vintage Airstream. Following in Great Southern's footsteps is The Bay, located across the street from Farm & Fire and North Beach Social, which serves up Southern- and Asian-inspired favorites and delicious sushi along with live music and events regularly. For specialty frozen drinks in Seaside, stop by Great Southern's b.f.f., a chic walk-up bar with a twist!

Fresh, local, and sustainable still define the Jim Shirley Enterprises brand across all its restaurants. Although native to Pensacola, Florida, Shirley's family grew up traveling with his Navy pilot father, and the chef's style draws inspiration from the New Ruralism movement, celebrating the proud farming history of the South and other traditionally rural areas to help create sustainable agriculture in today's more urban society. He has traveled the globe to learn about sustainable farm-to-table techniques and gain inspiration for his food and beverage menus. Still, he explains, "A huge influence on my career as a chef and restaurateur came from both of my grandmothers, who were the quintessential Southern cooks."

In a challenging industry, owning and operating six restaurants takes immense perseverance, but Shirley's tapestry of culinary greatness doesn't end there. He is also the co-owner of Great Southern Restaurants in Pensacola, which operates the Fish House, Atlas Oyster House, Jackson's Steakhouse, Angelena's Ristorante Italiano, 5 Sisters Blues Café, and Palafox House.

Along with creating great food and dining experiences, the Jim Shirley Enterprises mission places great emphasis on giving back to the community, state, and region. The chef is a board member and former president of the Florida Restaurant & Lodging Association and regularly makes appearances at charity functions such as the annual Seaside School Half Marathon Taste of the Race event, which Chef Emeril Lagasse hosts as a benefit for the Seaside Neighborhood School. He is the organizer of the Children's Home Society of Florida's annual fund-raiser called Soundside Splendor in Pensacola. Shirley is also involved with Southern Foodways Alliance, a member-supported nonprofit organization based at the University of Mississippi's Center for the Study of Southern Culture. Its mission is to document, study, and explore the diverse food cultures of the changing American South with the hope of "driving a more progressive future by leading conversations that challenge existing constructs, shape perspectives, and foster meaningful discussions."

59

Chef Jim Shirley

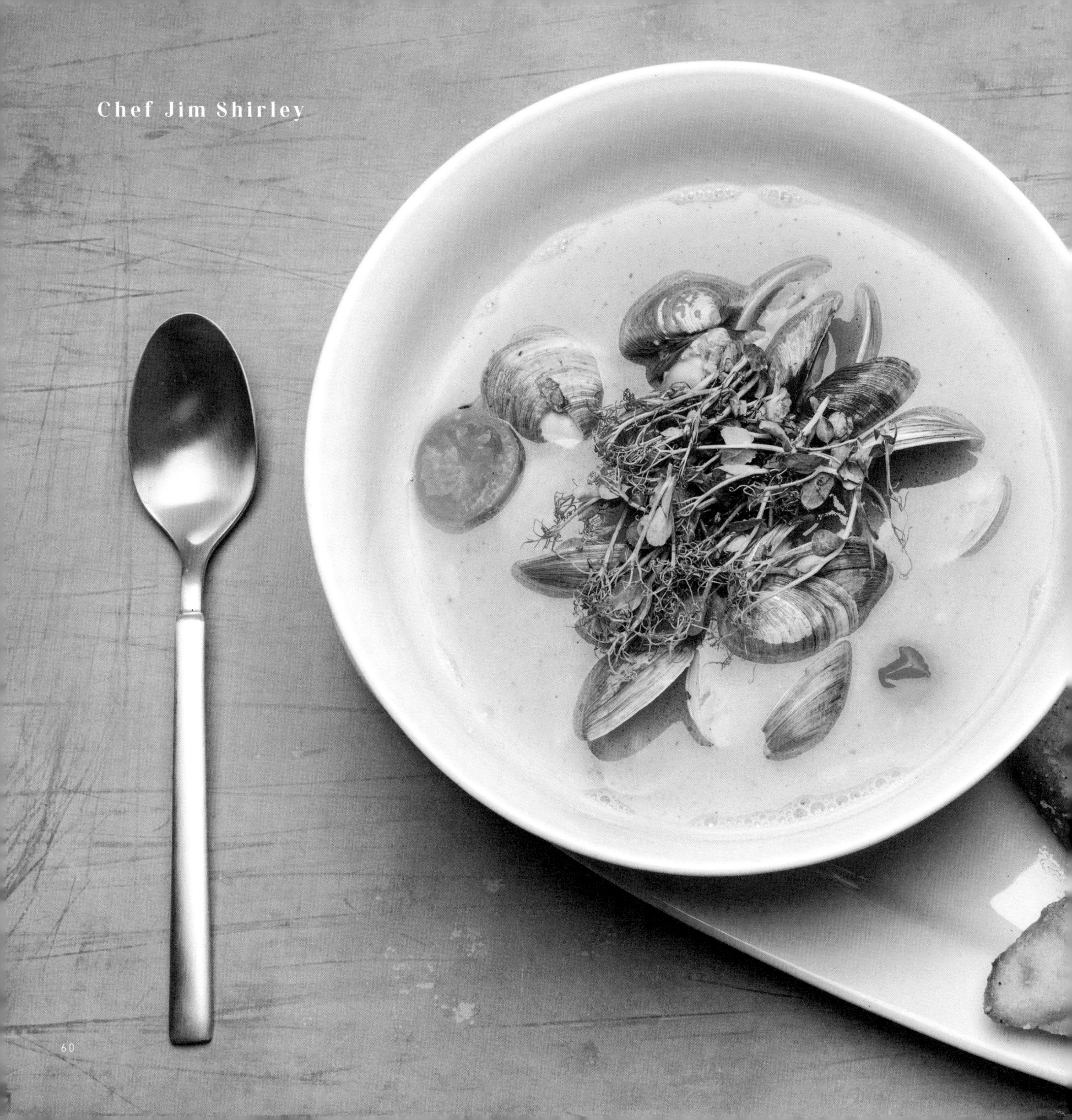

His efforts have not gone unnoticed, as his restaurants have racked up awards and accolades over the past twenty-five years since Shirley opened his first Pensacola restaurant, Madison's Diner (named for his eldest daughter, who now holds a leadership position with Chef Jim Shirley Enterprises). In addition to being asked to participate in six James Beard Foundation dinners, his signature Grits à Ya Ya dish has been named Florida's best Southern dish by *Florida Travel + Life magazine*. Shirley was invited to prepare it for over one thousand people on Capitol Hill in Washington, DC, as part of Taste of the South, organized by US Congressman Jeff Miller of Florida. Shirley and his team have been invited to cook meals for multiple Florida government officials and events in Tallahassee. Shirley also received the 2020 Shining Example Award – Epicurean Partner from the Southeast Tourism Society.

In 2022, the chef and his team headed to the Big Apple with Visit South Walton to participate in Food Network's fifteenth New York City Wine & Food Festival, cooking several dishes from Chef Jim's restaurants. Great Southern Café was also recently named winner of a 2022 *Wine Spectator* award—its ninth year earning this distinction.

"There's always something new happening at our restaurants," Chef Jim expounds. "We're always happy to represent Florida and South Walton to a global audience at these events and to offer our locals creative and delicious menu items and specialty cocktails year-round. We're grateful to be part of so many family traditions in South Walton and to tell the story of Florida food through all our restaurants and events."

For those who might not be visiting the Gulf Coast of Northwest Florida anytime soon, Shirley's cookbook, *Good Grits! (Southern Boy Cooks)*, offers a sampling of his signature recipes and stories from his first fifteen years in the restaurant business. It is available on Amazon.

Tuna Poke

By Chef Jim Shirley

For the Quick Pickling Juice

YIELDS ONE PINT

- 2 cups rice vinegar
- ¼ cup sugar
- 1 tablespoon ginger, minced
- 1 tablespoon soy sauce
- 1 tablespoon sesame oil
- 2 tablespoons toasted white sesame seeds

DIRECTIONS

Whisk all ingredients together until the sugar dissolves. Note: Pickling juice can be used three times.

For the Poke Dressing

- ¼ cup soy sauce
- ¼ cup fresh ginger, peeled and chopped
- ¼ cup cilantro, chopped
- ½ tablespoon garlic, chopped
- ¼ cup rice vinegar
- ½ tablespoon white sugar
- 1 cup oil
- ¼ cup toasted sesame seeds
- ¼ cup green onion, sliced very thin

DIRECTIONS

Blend soy sauce, ginger, cilantro, garlic, rice vinegar, white sugar, and oil until smooth. Transfer to a bowl and mix in sesame seeds and green onion.

For the Spicy Mayo

- 1 cup Duke's Mayonnaise
- ¼ cup Sriracha sauce
- ¼ tablespoon soy sauce
- ¼ tablespoon sesame oil

DIRECTIONS

Whisk all ingredients together in a bowl.

For the Tuna Poke

- 1 pound cubed ahi tuna
- Poke dressing
- Thinly sliced cucumber (to taste)
- Quick pickling juice
- Diced mango
- Carrot shreds
- ½ pound imitation crabmeat
- Spicy mayo
- 1 avocado
- Mixed greens
- Lime juice
- Salt
- Sriracha sauce

DIRECTIONS

Marinate cucumber and carrot shreds in the quick pickling juice for 1 hour. Thoroughly mix cubed ahi tuna with poke dressing. Shred the imitation crabmeat and mix it with spicy mayo. Mash the avocado and mix it with lime juice and salt to taste.

The poke ingredients can be served separately so guests can build their own or blend and portion out. Enjoy!

Turmeric Sour

By Chef Jim Shirley

Ingredients

- 1 ¾ ounces turmeric gin
- ¼ ounce amaretto
- ¾ ounce simple syrup
- 1 ounce sour mix
- 1 egg white
- Peychaud's Bitters, for garnish
- 1 toasted orange peel, for garnish

Directions

Shake the first five ingredients together and garnish with Peychaud's Bitters and a toasted orange peel. Cheers!

65

Duck Calls from
Great Southern Café

"

We're grateful to be part of so many family traditions in South Walton and to tell the story of Florida food.

—CHEF JIM SHIRLEY

Meet Me at The Red Bar

A neon rouge glow washes over the patrons, staff, and local musicians who frequent the famous Red Bar and Piccolo Restaurant in Grayton Beach, Florida. The eclectic watering hole and eatery was first opened in 1995 by Oli Petit, a Belgian restaurateur whose father, Louis, instilled in him the love and knowledge of the business. Covered in memorabilia and eccentric art on every wall, ceiling, and available surface, the Red Bar has been serving seafood favorites and cold drinks to visitors and locals ever since, except during a brief hiatus following a devastating electrical fire in February of 2019. Fans around the country were heartbroken, but Petit and his family reopened the doors in July of 2020. The new and improved space, designed with the help of A BOHEME architecture, Luke & Blue's construction, and O'Connell & Associates engineering, is certainly cause for elation. Eliciting much praise (and relief), the landmark's funky soul was perfectly preserved, and the Red Bar rocks on.

An Intimate Dining Table
Good Food, Friends, *and* Conversation

When Chef Nikhil Abuvala opened Roux 30a in Grayton Beach, Florida, in 2013, the small yet elegant dining space was the source of intrigue for many curious locals and visitors alike. "Is this a restaurant?" or "When is it open?" became familiar refrains for those who just happened upon the unassuming facade or found it listed on Google under nearby dining options. A decade later, Roux has become a perfect example of the phrase "If you know, you know."

Abuvala and his team specialize in private dinners and small events, ensuring a personal touch and intimate experience for all who enter the warmly lit, twelve-hundred-square-foot dining space with family-style tables and bar seating at the chef's counter. Fine wine is never in short supply here, with pairings specially selected for each meal or event. Patrons can rent out Roux 30a for special occasions or hire Chef Abuvala and his team to cook in their homes or cater meals. Alternatively, diners can get the full Roux 30a experience by reserving a spot for one of the restaurant's six-course dinners, which happen most nights per week, or for one of its special events, such as Chef Abuvala's Around the World dinner series featuring global-inspired cuisine.

Roux 30a started with a few of these events each month and has evolved into a popular local dining experience that promises world-class food and a lively yet exclusive atmosphere. When seated at the table or bar for dinner or even Roux's "Snack Hour," one gets the sense they're part of a private club or, as the team thinks of it, a family. The rise of Roux 30a spurred more success for Abuvala, who opened Nanbu Noodle Bar—a Japanese-style ramen and sushi restaurant with distinct Southern influences—in Grayton Beach in 2019 and The Daytrader Tiki Bar & Restaurant in Seaside, Florida, in 2023. Both were received warmly and with much fanfare. Nanbu's success also led to expanding with a pop-up in the City Food Hall at Destin Commons.

In addition to knowing how to create hype around his restaurants, Abuvala is undoubtedly one of the area's most talented and in-demand chefs. His Indian heritage and Southern upbringing combine with his professional training at the Culinary Institute of America and under top chefs, including Dean James Max and more. "My love of cooking has been with me as early as I can remember, standing on a chair and rolling out fresh Indian flatbreads with my grandmother on a counter too tall for me to reach otherwise," Abuvala says. "The way she moved about the kitchen, like a general of an army commanding spices and herbs, sparked a passion for food in me that is unmatched."

Along with his team, Abuvala focuses on modern coastal cuisine at Roux 30a, where the open-concept kitchen and beautiful presentation truly bring the guest experience to the next level. Whether you're on vacation, have lived in the area for years and never visited, or are already a loyal fan, this family table is waiting!

Indian-Spiced Prawns and Saffron Grits

By Chef Nikhil Abuvala, Roux 30a

SERVES 6

For the Grits

INGREDIENTS

- 6 cups water
- 1 ½ cups stone ground grits (use traditional here, not quick grits)
- 2 teaspoons kosher salt
- ½ cup melted ghee
- 3 green cardamom pods, crushed
- ½ teaspoon cumin seed
- 6 curry leaves
- 1 serrano chili, minced (seeds removed if you want less spice)
- ½-inch knob ginger, minced
- 3 cloves of garlic, minced
- ½ teaspoon saffron
- ½ teaspoon garam masala
- ½ teaspoon granulated sugar
- ¼ cup full-fat yogurt
- Juice of half a lime
- Salt to taste

DIRECTIONS

In a pot, bring 6 cups of water to a boil. Add salt. Whisk the grits in slowly to combine, and turn the heat down to low. Cook for 15 to 20 minutes, stirring often to prevent burning or clumping, until the grits are tender but still have a bite.

In a separate saucepan, heat ghee on medium heat. Add cardamom, cumin seed, and curry leaves. Fry spices for 1 minute in the ghee, then add serrano, ginger, and garlic. Fry for 2 minutes, then turn off the heat. Add saffron, garam masala, and sugar to ghee and let sit for 5 minutes. Stir well to combine and pour into the pot of grits. Add yogurt, lime juice, and salt to taste. Serve with Indian-Spiced Prawns.

For the Prawns

INGREDIENTS

- 2 tablespoons ghee
- ½ medium yellow onion, diced
- ½ teaspoon cumin seed
- ¼ teaspoon black mustard seed
- ½ inch knob of ginger, minced
- ½ serrano chili, minced (seeds removed if you want less spice)
- 3 cloves of garlic, minced
- ½ teaspoon cayenne pepper
- ½ teaspoon turmeric
- ½ teaspoon ground coriander
- ½ teaspoon ground cumin
- ⅛ teaspoon asafoetida (optional)
- 1 teaspoon salt
- 1 14 ½-ounce can crushed tomatoes (Muir Glen fire-roasted crushed tomatoes are our favorite)
- 1 teaspoon sugar
- 1 ½ pounds extra-large prawns or shrimp (peeled and deveined)
- ¼ cup heavy cream
- ¼ cup chicken stock (or water)
- 1 teaspoon garam masala
- Cilantro to garnish

DIRECTIONS

Add ghee to a large saucepan on medium-high heat. Add diced onion and cook until the onion starts to turn brown. Turn heat down to medium and add cumin seed and mustard seed, cook for 1 minute. Add ginger, garlic, serrano chili, and spices. Cook for 2 minutes. Add crushed tomatoes and sugar, then stir. Cook for 5 to 10 minutes until most of the liquid evaporates, stirring often to prevent it from burning. Add prawns (or shrimp) to the tomato mixture. Cook for 2 to 3 minutes, stirring often until shrimp begins to turn pink. Add heavy cream, chicken stock, and garam masala. Cook for an additional 2 to 3 minutes until combined. Serve over Saffron Grits and garnish with cilantro. Please enjoy!

The Essence of Life
Breaking Bread Together

When proprietors Dave Rauschkolb and Chef Phil McDonald created Black Bear Bread Co. in 2016, it was a farmers' market staple in Seaside, Florida, providing fresh sourdough bread, baguettes, and other baked goods. The bakery, operating out of Rauschkolb's catering kitchen for Bud & Alley's Waterfront Restaurant, was named for the Florida black bears who are well known to locals. (The bears used to "dumpster dive" for scraps and sourdough when the bakers were experimenting and had yet to name the enterprise.) When the opportunity arose to open a restaurant in nearby Grayton Beach, Black Bear Bread Co. evolved into a modern café styled after those in Brooklyn, New York, where McDonald lived for a year before returning to the Gulf Coast.

With a second location in Miramar Beach, a third in Seaside, and a wine bar expansion at the Grayton location for private events, Black Bear has become a favorite among locals and tourists alike for its homemade bread and pastries, Stumptown Coffee, lunch items, organic wines, artisanal cheeses, and friendly atmosphere.

"I wanted to make bread the right way, naturally leavened," McDonald explains. After making his own starter from yeast that was "born" at the Bud & Alley's Pizza Bar in Seaside years before, it was time to experiment to create the perfect sourdough. "I made fifty to sixty loaves that were horrible—but they kept getting better."

Now, Black Bear Bread Co. is a staple for visitors and locals who stop by its three stylish locations for homemade breakfast pastries, bagels, biscuit sandwiches, oatmeal, granola, grain bowls, tartines, and so much more. Stumptown Coffee Roasters of Portland, Oregon, supplies guests with their caffeine fix through barista creations and drip coffee. The menu also offers local and regional craft beers, wines by the glass, and other specialty beverages. Lunch specials are always worth checking out and range from sandwiches to salads and fresh seafood. McDonald says his philosophy is "to make simple, clean, fun food from scratch, using seasonal offerings."

Chef Phil McDonald

Key Lime Croissants

By Pastry Chef Kara Enache, Black Bear Bread Co.

YIELDS 6 CROISSANTS

Ingredients

FOR THE CURD

- 5 egg yolks
- 23 ounces condensed milk
- 6 ½ ounces key lime juice

FOR THE MERINGUE

- 5 egg whites
- 4 ounces granulated sugar

FOR THE PASTRY

- 6 croissants, baked
- 1 lime
- ¼ cup graham cracker crumbs

Directions

FOR THE CURD:

Mix all ingredients together and refrigerate until needed. Curd can be made the day before.

FOR THE PASTRY:

Split open croissants horizontally. Carefully fill with a scant ½ cup of key lime curd. (Curd will be thin, but will soak into the croissant.) Close the croissant gently and top with a spoonful of curd. Allow the curd to drip down from the top onto the sides. Bake at 300°F for 6 to 10 minutes, until the curd is set and just starting to brown around the edges of the drips. Keep croissants on the pan and set aside.

FOR THE MERINGUE:

Whip egg whites on high speed until foamy. With the mixer on, slowly stream in granulated sugar. Whip to a stiff peak (meringue is smooth and shiny, and tips can stand straight up or with a small curl at the very top when beaters are lifted).

Immediately place meringue into a piping bag fitted with your choice of tip and pipe onto the top of the baked croissants. Alternately, dollop meringue onto the croissants and swirl around to create different designs.

Place croissants back into the oven and bake until the meringue is golden brown (about 5 to 7 minutes). Or, using a torch, brown meringue until set and golden. Garnish meringue with lime slices and a sprinkle of graham cracker crumbs. Enjoy!

"

Coffee is a way of life.

A Legacy of Good
Community, Consistency, *and a* Calling

Locals and visitors alike agree that when it comes to dining along Scenic Highway 30-A, this place has it all. A leader in the restaurant community along Scenic Highway 30-A in Northwest Florida since 1995, Café Thirty-A is a go-to spot for casual fine dining, an extensive wine list, martini specials, and memorable desserts. General manager David Kessler and executive chef Tim Williams are known for their "consistently delicious" approach that keeps locals and vacationers coming back time and again.

Whether guests stop by the bar for 'Tini Nights (six-dollar martinis every Tuesday and Thursday!) or to have dinner in the expansive, airy main dining room, the food and drinks are always exceptional. The menu offers a variety for everyone, with fresh seafood, steaks, pizza, and more, along with daily specials and a fantastic wine list. Café Thirty-A's coastal atmosphere and beautiful decor are a great setting for private events, and they provide off-site catering.

Café Thirty-A's late owner, Harriet Crommelin, who passed away in February of 2023, was known not only for fostering community through the restaurant but also for doing good for those in need. Crommelin and Café Thirty-A have given back to the area that supports the restaurant wholeheartedly by donating to nonprofits and charitable events throughout the year. Their most significant effort is the annual Café Thirty-A Christmas Charity Ball, which is a way to give back, bring people together, and celebrate the holidays all at once. The 2022 event raised a record $50,000 for the featured nonprofit, Caring & Sharing of South Walton, which provides food and financial assistance to area families and individuals in need. The event included a silent auction with items donated by dozens of local and regional businesses.

"This is always a special event for us and our staff to host each year," Crommelin said of the Christmas ball. "Seeing our friends and long-time patrons come out to support a cause that is near and dear to our hearts proves that this community believes in giving and paying it forward even when it's the busiest time of the year."

Crommelin's passing left a hole in the hearts of many, but her legacy lives on through Café Thirty-A's fantastic food and generous charity, nourishing friends and family in both body and spirit.

Don't miss 'Tini Night at Café Thirty-A!

81

Jumbo Lump Crab Cakes

By Café Thirty-A

YIELDS 2 TO 4 CRAB CAKES

Ingredients

- 2 pounds jumbo lump crabmeat
- ¼ cup mayonnaise
- 2 ounces (about ¼ cup) sour cream
- 1 tablespoon whole-grain mustard
- 1 egg
- 2 ounces (about ¼ cup) scallions, chopped
- 1 teaspoon Florida Bay Seasoning
- ¼ teaspoon salt
- Panko crumbs, as needed
- Butter or extra-virgin olive oil, as needed

Directions

Pick through the crabmeat to clean it of shells and debris. Be careful not to break up lumps. Combine all ingredients except for the crab in a mixing bowl. Add the crab and enough panko crumbs to make the mix formable. Use a small cake ring to shape the cakes.

Melt a little butter or add oil to a sauté pan over medium-high heat and sauté the crab cakes until golden brown, about 4 to 5 minutes on each side. Serve with simple greens and remoulade or Joe's mustard sauce, and enjoy this Gulf Coast classic!

Thirty-A Old Fashioned

By Café Thirty-A

Ingredients

- 2 ounces bourbon, such as Michter's Small Batch
- ¼ ounce blood orange bitters
- 1 splash simple syrup
- 1 large ice cube
- Orange twist, for garnish

Directions

In a cocktail mixing glass, combine bourbon, blood orange bitters, and simple syrup with a little ice and stir for about 20 to 30 seconds until well combined. Place the large ice cube in a rocks glass and strain the cocktail over it. Garnish with an orange twist and sip slowly to savor this iconic cocktail.

A Gulf-Front Landmark

Serving Local Favorites *in* Seaside

Ask hardcore fans of Seaside, Florida, and they'll tell you that catching a sunset from the Gulf-front rooftop of Bud & Alley's is a quintessential experience during any visit. Many locals swear by the crab cakes here as a dinnertime favorite, while others love stopping by for a relaxing lunch with a view of turquoise water stretching to the horizon. For owner Dave Rauschkolb, one of Seaside's original pioneers who opened the waterfront restaurant with business and surfing partner Scott Witcoski in 1986, Bud & Alley's is a legacy, a place full of stories and connections.

The pair of twenty-four-year-old entrepreneurs started the iconic eatery when only about a dozen homes were in Seaside. They named it after two—perhaps equally iconic—animals: Seaside founders Robert and Daryl Davis's dachshund, Bud, and Scott's cat, Alley. Rauschkolb reminisces, "We were on a deadline to put a listing in the phone book and throwing out ideas when Robert's secretary said she liked the name Bud & Alley's. It seemed crazy at the time,

but it was the perfect personification of what we would become—a casual, unpretentious eatery with great food."

Bud & Alley's has seen much evolution since its humble beginnings. Its offerings include the adjacent Pizza Bar and Taco Bar, which are crowd favorites for families who visit year after year. An extensive renovation completed in 2021 brought Pizza Bar into the street level of the building, with a café terrace next to the beautiful Krier Plaza. Meanwhile, the rooftop was expanded to include another deck overlooking the heart of the town.

Equating the restaurant staff to part of his family, Rauschkolb says he has seen people from all walks of life come work for him and springboard to grander culinary careers. Others are former employees whose children worked at Bud & Alley's as their first summer job. Undoubtedly, this place will continue as a family tradition for locals and visitors alike for years to come.

Restaurateur Dave
Rauschkolb and Chef
David Bishop

Barbecued Head-On Shrimp

By Chef David Bishop, Bud & Alley's Waterfront Restaurant

SERVES 1

Ingredients

- 1 tablespoon all-purpose seasoning, such as Everglades Seasoning
- 1 tablespoon cayenne pepper
- 1 tablespoon celery salt
- 1 tablespoon vegetable oil
- ¼ cup sliced andouille sausage
- 6 large shrimp, peeled, head and tail left on
- 2 cloves garlic, sliced
- 1 sprig fresh rosemary
- 1 cup white wine
- 3 ounces unsalted butter, cut into small pieces
- Grilled bread* for serving

Directions

FOR THE BARBECUE SEASONING:

Mix the all-purpose seasoning, cayenne pepper, and celery salt in an airtight container.

FOR THE SHRIMP:

Heat a large skillet over medium-high heat. Add the vegetable oil, sausage, and shrimp. Cook for one minute, and then turn the shrimp over and continue cooking. Add the garlic and rosemary sprig and cook for another minute. Pour in the wine to deglaze, and then add the butter and a half teaspoon of the barbecue seasoning. Reduce the heat to medium and swirl the pan to incorporate the butter. Taste and add a half teaspoon more of the seasoning, if needed. (Reserve the remaining seasoning in an airtight container for another use.)

Transfer the shrimp and sausage to a serving bowl and garnish with a slice of grilled Tuscan-style bread. *Bud & Alley's proudly serves naturally leavened artisanal sourdough bread from Black Bear Bread Co.

Airstream Row

Scenic Highway 30-A is full of iconic eateries, but the New Urbanist town of Seaside has a truly unique experience with its collection of vintage Airstream trailers–turned–food trucks. Affectionately nicknamed Airstream Row, this line of eateries has everything, from sweet and savory snacks to gourmet sandwiches, snow cones, barbecue, and health food options. Locals and visitors alike line up along the sidewalk at the south end of Central Square for their favorites, like grilled cheese from The Meltdown on 30A and classic American hot dogs from Wild Bill's Beach Dogs. A Seaside staple for kids of all ages is Frost Bites, whose sweet frozen treats are perfect for beating the heat. Airstream Row is an incredibly popular fixture in South Walton and a great one-stop foodie destination with something for everyone!

"

I never get tired of going to Bud & Alley's. I love the sunset, and I see faces I've seen for decades.

—DAVE RAUSCHKOLB, *VIE* MAGAZINE

Crab Cake from
Bud & Alley's

Alys Beach

"Idyllic" is one of our favorite ways to describe the high-end resort community of Alys Beach, Florida. Situated on the Gulf of Mexico on Scenic Highway 30-A, this New Urbanist beach town is home to globally inspired architecture, world-class restaurants, unique shops, and incredible events. A day spent exploring here is a day spent in paradise.

A Life Defined
Dine in Paradise

Within the white walls of Alys Beach, Florida, and flowing out onto its green spaces, pocket parks, architecturally framed landscapes, pedestrian paths, and pristine white-sand beaches, friends and families gather. Food and drink are central to bringing people together in a town designed for connection and creating community over shared spaces and festivities. Homeowners and guests eat together, celebrate, nourish their bodies, entertain, build fellowship, prepare and share meals, and connect over the elements upon which true hospitality and gracious living are based.

For Alys Beach, food and beverage programming is essential to realizing the overall vision for the town. The culinary team in this idyllic resort community on the Gulf curates experiences—from the public venue at NEAT Bottle Shop and Tasting Room to the private venues for rental guests and owners (Caliza Restaurant, ZUMA Café, and Beach Food & Beverage Delivery Service) and the owner-exclusive Beach Club. A collection of fully realized menus incorporates the global heritage and knowledge of the team and its audience, all within a pervading Southern tradition. Seasonal ingredients and flavors inform these menus, complemented by a dynamic beverage program of craft beers and cocktails, small-batch spirits, and refined wine lists.

The attention to quality and craft within Alys Beach's food and beverage offerings extends into private tastings, dinner services, and events ranging from small and intimate affairs to large-scale festivals. Food and drink are integral to the Alys Beach experience—to a Life Defined—including cooking demos, special gatherings, holiday meal delivery services for owners, private in-home tastings, a beautifully themed Supper Club Series, and multifaceted individual events comprising each of the town's signature festivals.

The overall food scene in Alys Beach continues to expand, with favorites such as George's and Raw & Juicy joined by The Citizen, Fonville Press Market Café, Holiday Cafe, and the new Charlie's Delights. Alys Beach's Town Center charts a path of excellence in quality hospitality, extending the Alys experience to the larger community through good food, great drinks, and a warm welcome.

Beverage manager Austin Doiron, chef de cuisine Renato Falconi, and executive chef Drew Dzejak

Roasted Gulf Grouper

with Quinoa Tabbouleh, Carrot-Parsnip Puree, Baby Greens, Radish, Tomato, and Pickled Onions

By Alys Beach

SERVINGS: 4

Ingredients

- 4 6-ounce portions Gulf grouper
- ¼ cup canola oil
- Espelette pepper
- 2 carrots
- 2 parsnips
- 2 ounces butter
- 8 ounces assorted baby lettuce
- 1 candy cane radish, peeled and thinly sliced
- 8 baby radishes with tops
- 12 golden grape tomatoes, split
- ¼ cup lemon juice
- ¼ cup olive oil
- 1 red onion, julienne
- 1 cup red wine vinegar
- 3 tablespoons pickling spice
- 1 tablespoon sugar
- 1 cup red quinoa, rinsed
- 8 mint leaves, chopped
- ½ bunch parsley, chopped
- Zest and juice of 2 lemons
- 1 vine ripened tomato, seeded and diced
- 4 tablespoons olive oil

Directions

FOR THE TABBOULEH:

Bring 2 quarts of salted water to a boil. Drop rinsed quinoa into the boiling water and simmer for about 15 minutes or until the quinoa looks to have sprouted. Strain and cool down. Once cooled, mix quinoa, mint, parsley, lemon juice and zest, tomato, and olive oil. Season with salt and pepper and set aside.

FOR THE SALAD:

Start by making the pickled onions. Bring the red wine vinegar to a boil with pickling spice and sugar. Blanch the red onions for 3 to 4 minutes, then remove from the liquid and allow the onions and the liquid to cool. Once both are cool, combine them again and allow to sit overnight under refrigeration. To make the salad, in a large mixing bowl, combine lettuce, radishes, golden tomatoes, pickled onions, olive oil, and lemon juice. Season with salt and pepper.

FOR THE CARROT-PARSNIP PUREE:

Peel the carrots and parsnips and cut into 1-inch pieces. In a medium pot, cover the carrots and parsnips with water and bring to a boil. Season water with salt and simmer until vegetables are tender. Once tender, strain, put in a blender, and add butter. Puree until smooth. Season to taste.

FOR THE GROUPER:

Preheat the oven to 400°F. Place a large sauté pan over high heat. Pour the canola in and allow the oil to warm. Season fish with salt and Espelette pepper. Place fish in the pan and sear for 5 to 6 minutes until a golden crust has formed. Flip the fish, place in the oven, and bake for 10 minutes. Enjoy!

Shibuya Martini

By Alys Beach

Ingredients

- ¼ ounce Pierre Ferrand Dry Curaçao
- 2 ounces Mizu Lemongrass Shochu
- ¼ ounce Thatcher's Organic Cucumber Liqueur
- ½ ounce lemon juice
- Ginger ale to top

Directions

Shake all ingredients (except ginger ale) with ice and strain into a martini glass. Top with ginger ale. The addition of fresh lemon juice gives the drink brightness and life, and a topper of ginger ale complements the curaçao and adds some texture. Cheers!

Savor the moments that

Outstanding in the
Field alfresco dinner at
Kaiya Beach Resort

take your breath away.

Citizens of the World
Creating *a* Modern Coastal Tavern

"I think food plays such a special part in our lives. There is something very real about the idea of creating community through food," says Jeremy Walton, the creator and owner of Quest Hospitality Concepts, proprietors of The Citizen and the newly reimagined Fonville Press in the idyllic town of Alys Beach, Florida. After serving as the vice president of resort operations there since 2014, Jeremy found himself in the unique position to branch out to open his own restaurants in Alys Beach with the help of his wife, Angela.

Shortly thereafter came the inception of The Citizen, a modern coastal tavern in the heart of the resort community. Working with the Alys Beach team and the town planners at Khoury Vogt Architects on the restaurant's design, Quest Hospitality sought to bring a sophisticated, city-inspired dining experience to the area.

"The vision was to develop a design-forward restaurant where the experience was centered around three things: a big, beautiful bar, an immersive raw bar, and a wood-burning hearth in an open kitchen," says Jeremy. Of course, a menu featuring fresh Gulf seafood and oysters from local and regional purveyors was also a must. Still, international influences and ingredients also play into the restaurant's ethos and its patrons as being "citizens" of the world, not just the Gulf Coast. "Given that so many great food cities are situated near coastlines, we wanted to draw inspiration for the menus from any and all of those coastal cuisines."

Storytelling is also a focus at The Citizen, from the travel-influenced decor to the quotes printed on each menu and its team's curated approach to social media. It all melds to create an experience diners feel they could have in a seaside bar along the Mediterranean, a dockside café in San Francisco, or an upscale Caribbean resort. Navy, white, and gold interiors evoke the nautical feeling, while rattan seating and a few warm wood accents add a laid-back luxury vibe indicative of Alys Beach. "While we wanted the restaurant to be beautiful, we did not want it to be formal," Jeremy reiterates. Ample seating, at both the bar and the raw bar, further augments the sense that this is a gathering spot for lively conversation and good times, not stuffy special occasions only. Along with its sister restaurant and market across the green, Fonville Press, The Citizen is poised to lead Alys Beach's restaurant scene into a bright future ahead.

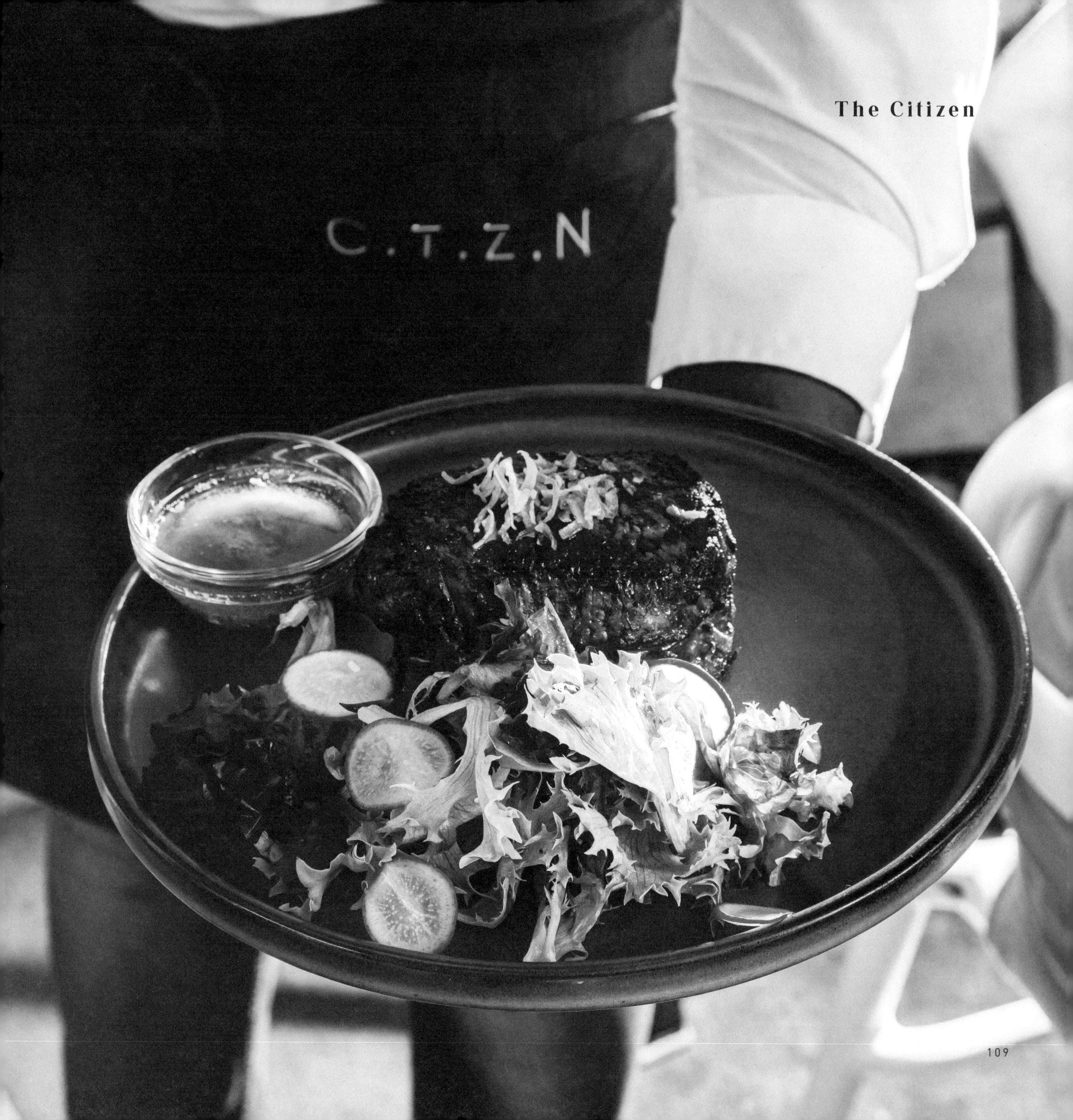
C.T.Z.N

Jalisco Swizzle

By The Citizen

Refreshing and minty, the swizzle hails from the long-standing West Indian tradition that paved the way for tiki. Named after the swizzle stick, a long-pronged stick used for mixing the drink, this is a riff on the classic Queen's Park Swizzle, replacing rum with tequila.

Ingredients

- 2 ounces Cimarron Blanco Tequila
- ¾ ounce lime juice
- ½ ounce mint simple syrup
- Muddled mint
- Angostura bitters
- Mint bundle, for garnish
- Crushed ice

Directions

Add 5 to 7 mint leaves and mint syrup to a highball glass and gently press mint with a muddler. Add tequila and lime juice, then insert your swizzle stick. Fill the glass with crushed ice, swizzle until all ingredients are mixed, and top with more crushed ice. Float bitters on top. Garnish with a mint sprig, and enjoy. *¡Salud!*

Gulf Shrimp Bisque

By Chef Drew Dzejak, The Citizen

SERVES 8

Ingredients

- 3 tablespoons butter
- 2 medium onions, diced
- 6 ribs celery, diced
- 1 pound shrimp shells
- 4 fresh bay leaves
- 3 tablespoons flour
- 3 ounces tomato paste
- ½ cup cognac
- 2 cups clam juice
- 2 cups heavy cream
- 1 teaspoon Worcestershire sauce
- 1 teaspoon hot sauce
- Salt and white pepper to taste
- 16 large Gulf shrimp, peeled and deveined

Directions

In a heavy-bottom Dutch oven, melt butter over medium-high heat. Add onions and celery, sweat with no color to soften vegetables, and cook for 5 minutes.

Turn the heat up to high to add shrimp shells and bay leaves. Toast shells until they turn a red color, then add flour. Mix in flour, then quickly add in tomato paste. Toast the tomato paste and shells to develop a deep red color. Deglaze with cognac and allow the alcohol to cook out for 3 to 4 minutes. (Chef's note: make sure to stir constantly so the tomato paste does not burn).

Add clam juice and bring to a boil. Simmer for 10 minutes, then add cream, Worcestershire, and hot sauce. Allow soup to simmer for 20 minutes, and season with salt and pepper.

In a large blender and working in batches, puree the soup and strain through a fine mesh strainer. To garnish, season Gulf shrimp with salt and pepper and either grill or sear in a sauté pan. Serve with fresh bread, and enjoy!

The Citizen

Peanut Butter Banana
Trifle from The Citizen

Honestly Organic
The Evolution *of* Raw & Juicy

"I want to help farmers get their food out of the fields and onto our tables," says Jenifer Kuntz, the owner and visionary of Raw & Juicy organic juice bar and café in Alys Beach, Florida. "In the end, it comes down to what the market demands. Raw & Juicy is here because our community demands good, wholesome food."

The science of eating organic, sustainable whole foods—mainly fruits, vegetables, nuts, and legumes—as a crucial part of overall human wellness has been proven and greatly expanded upon in the past few decades. The mission at Raw & Juicy incorporates good health with a great love for life and nature. Kuntz, born in Georgia, grew up near Anchorage, Alaska, and spent most of her days outdoors, hiking and playing with her dogs. As an adult she cites yoga and dance as other great balancing forces in her overall wellness. Twenty years after landing on the Gulf Coast of Florida amid white-sand beaches, flatwoods trails, and rare coastal dune lakes, Kuntz is happy to have found both a home for her nature-loving self and a warm reception for her thoughtful business.

Kuntz opened Raw & Juicy in 2008 in her remodeled 1966 Land Yacht Airstream along Seaside's Airstream Row on Scenic Highway 30-A. The café and its culinary team became local and visitor favorites. "We introduced organic and seasonal food as a way of eating and put vegan and vegetarian food on the map on 30-A," she says. "We also introduced raw food and acai bowls to the area in 2008— until the farm we bought from in Brazil couldn't keep up with our demand and ran out of acai!" They've since found another source.

The café's efforts inspired other local businesses to carry grass-fed beef and offer vegan options, cultivating an artisan food culture that has since blossomed exponentially. Kuntz led the revival of the Saturday farmers' market in Seaside, Florida, harking back to the New Urbanist town's early days. "Seaside cofounder Daryl Davis taught me the power of incubating business through the farmers' market, as she did with the original market in 1981. We are honored to have helped foster the growth of many now-thriving local purveyors and restaurants." These include Black Bear Bread Co., Chanticleer Eatery, JC's Gourmet, Sweet Henrietta's, Noli South, and NaturBaker. The success of the Seaside Farmers Market inspired farmers' markets throughout South Walton, preserving farmland and educating people on the importance of connecting to their food, local farmers, and the seasons.

In 2019, the iconic 30-A eatery moved to an equally iconic location in nearby Alys Beach, the former home of Fonville Press (which has since reopened just down the street). With a beautiful outdoor dining space and sidewalk café tables, the local favorite has been a perfect addition to the town, holding bespoke farm-to-table wine dinners, hosting events for 30A Wine Festival and 30A Songwriters Festival, and, of course, providing visitors with their daily organic coffee, tea, fresh juice, smoothies, and more.

Raw & Juicy also has a production kitchen, located in nearby Point Washington, where the café's pressed organic juices are made. Its state-of-the-art juicer is a behemoth and truly a sight to behold, and the team works long hours to create the café's rotation of signature juices, updated daily. The café menu includes delicious breakfast items, such as organic coffee, avocado toast, and omelets. Lunch offerings keep visitors coming back for more with a delicious lentil-beet burger, open-faced sandwiches, and a savory kale salad. Dinner is a relatively new offering, available Thursdays through Saturdays by reservation—to accommodate the harvesting of fresh ingredients. "Since our inception, Raw & Juicy has been dedicated to local, fresh ingredients," Kuntz shares. "Building on that dedication, we're excited to welcome guests for dinner service, curated by chef Michael Sichel in collaboration with local and regional farmers and fishermen."

It's no wonder the café has accumulated not only a vast following among locals and visitors but also numerous awards and accolades, including being named one of the top ten juice bars in the country by *USA Today*. Kuntz shares proudly, "We had humble beginnings in an Airstream trailer, but inspired by an ideology and some grit, we've been able to influence the food culture of an entire region."

Jenifer Lee Kuntz

Lacto-Fermented Meyer Lemons

By Raw & Juicy

Ingredients

- 10 Meyer lemons (enough to fill a quart jar when squished)
- 1–2 tablespoons Himalayan sea salt

Directions

Quarter 8 to 10 Meyer lemons from the top to the bottom and push them lightly toward the bottom of a quart jar to release some juice. Add a tablespoon of sea salt and continue to work the lemons lightly—do not press them too much, or you will release the oils from the rind and cause the ferment to become bitter.

You want the jar to be full to the top with lemons packed close together and the brine just above the lemons. If you do not have enough brine in the jar to cover the lemons, you'll need to make one by adding warm water and sea salt to a jar. Once the salt dissolves, add enough of the salt brine to the natural lemon juice brine to cover the lemons completely. The brine should be ⅛ of an inch below the lid.

Place the lid on the jar and leave it in a warm place out of direct sunlight for 2 weeks or more. You can check your lemons for desired taste and flavor; the longer they sit, the more flavorful they'll become.

Once fermented, these lemons become a probiotic powerhouse. Add the juice to warm water in the morning as a liver tonic, or enjoy the rind by removing the pith and chopping to top desserts (flan), put in smoothies, or enjoy on a salad. Place on fish, use in meat dishes, or dehydrate and turn into nourishing dust to create sauces.

Antioxidant Smoothie

By Raw & Juicy

Ingredients

- 1 frozen banana
- ½ cup frozen strawberries
- ½ cup frozen blueberries
- 1 slice fermented lemon rind
- 2 tablespoons goji berries
- 1 tablespoon maqui berry
- 1–2 cups milk of choice or water
- Pinch of Himalayan sea salt

Directions

Place all ingredients in a high-speed blender, blend until creamy, and enjoy!

"

We have the opportunity through hospitality to become a part of people's memories.

—JEREMY WALTON, *VIE* MAGAZINE

Blue Skies coffee from
Fonville Press Market Café

For The People
A Reimagined Icon Returns

When a beloved local café permanently closes its doors, it can be an emotional experience for the whole community. This was certainly the case for Fonville Press, a charming coffee shop and lunch destination in Alys Beach, Florida, whose closure in 2018 was met with sadness from those who loved it—but also with a sense of excitement for the future from those who hoped to see it return.

"It was obvious by the outpouring of support from locals and homeowners that there was a deep love for Fonville," says former Alys Beach vice president of resort operations and current owner of the reimagined Fonville Press, Jeremy Walton. "It had become a special and beloved brand. Because of that, we wanted to try to reimagine it and see it return. We understood we couldn't re-create the original Fonville. However, we wanted to honor it in a meaningful way and recapture its connection with people as a beloved gathering place."

He continues, "Markets, cafés, coffee shops, and bars all become these spaces where we gather and intersect with each other. We have the opportunity through hospitality to be a part of people's memories, and in these moments, those of us working in hospitality can add to these moments or take away from them. Our primary job is to build genuine relationships and create memorable experiences. At Fonville, we mean what our motto says:

For the People. We strive to uphold the same ethos and approach to hospitality at our sister restaurant and coastal tavern, The Citizen."

Wishing to expand on the experiences offered at Fonville, and thanks to having a much larger space to develop, its proprietors set out to open an all-in-one market, café, and bar. They worked closely with architect Anthony Vallee of McWhorter Vallee Design and interior designer Melissa Skowlund's team at Summer House Lifestyle to create an open yet inviting space. The warm, vibrant, fun, and colorful design is inspired by Southern California with a touch of Old Florida, featuring wood paneling, bright pinks, brass, tile, and lots of greenery. The exterior seating areas were critical elements of the design and guest experience, with the expansive bar wrapping from the interior to the outdoors.

The menu, helmed by executive chef Coleman Jernigan, is continuously evolving, picking up where the original Fonville left off with coffee, breakfast, and lunch staples. Dinner, a full bar, a bakery, a pizza oven, a rotisserie, grab-and-go options, and nightly take-home meals are also available in addition to the market and retail section. "We felt there was much more we could offer to create a versatile dining experience on 30-A with simple, fast, and delicious food in a design-forward space," says Walton.

Fonville Press

Fonville Press interiors designed in partnership with Melissa Skowlund of Summer House Lifestyle

127

Fonville Press

MARKET FONVILLE PRESS

Fonville offers a small market full of freshly baked bread, produce, and more groceries in addition to the café.

30A East End

Continuing east on our tour down Scenic Highway 30-A, the town centers of Seacrest Beach and Rosemary Beach boast unique experiences for both locals and tourists. Meanwhile, 30Avenue is a shopping and dining mecca at the intersection of 30A and Highway 98. Explore high-end restaurants, places to stay, and much more, all a short walk or bike ride away.

A Roof with a View
On Top *of the* World *in* Rosemary Beach

The Gulf of Mexico and its adjacent white-sand beaches are stunning year-round, and admiring them from above is always a treat. That's why the proprietors of Pescado in Rosemary Beach opted to turn the restaurant into one of South Walton's hottest rooftop dining destinations. With views including the Gulf, the beach, Western Green, and Main Street in the charming European-inspired town, it's a must-stop for anyone visiting the area and looking for a chic spot for dinner or drinks.

The wraparound bar has indoor and outdoor seating, while the rooftop is the best spot for dining alfresco with the best vistas. The menu, created by Chef John Engle and his team, alongside bar manager Tatiana Rotari, offers a range of items to please any palate. Fresh seafood is a given and a favorite among guests, including the robust seafood platter, pan-seared diver scallops, chef's ceviche, and, of course, the fish of the day, ranging from mouth-watering Gulf grouper to red snapper and more.

"Family style" is the name of the game at Pescado, where guests should consider ordering several starters, entrées, and sides so they can sample everything and enjoy it together. Dessert is a similarly delicious affair and shouldn't be skipped—after all, you shared your meal so you can justify the sweet ending, right? The seasonal crème brûlée selection is a great choice that always offers something new!

Don't forget the specialty craft beverages. Cocktails are a feature at the posh bar, a place one might expect to find in a metropolitan destination rather than this small New Urbanist village by the beach. The menu rotates with an impressive selection of spirits and cocktails, such as the Feelin' Peachy (Four Roses Bourbon, peach, vanilla, tarragon, and lemon) and the Kentexican (Corazón Añejo Tequila, Rittenhouse Rye, Amaro Nonino, honey, and bitters). Or, go for the Pescado Choice and let your mixologist whip up a beverage with the latest seasonal ingredients.

Downstairs in the heart of Rosemary Beach's shopping district, The Courtyard at Pescado is a special spot designed for larger groups and special events. Guests eighteen and older are invited to enjoy live music in the New Orleans–inspired lounge, with craft cocktails, wine, and beer available for patrons twenty-one and up. In addition, The Courtyard is available to rent for rehearsal dinners, birthdays, and more. Pescado also hosts a range of wine dinners, cocktail classes, and other events throughout the year.

The view of Rosemary Beach and the Gulf from Pescado's southern deck

Clams and Mussels
with coconut curry broth,
cherry tomatoes, ginger,
basil, and a grilled baguette
from Pescado

> ❝
>
> I'm not sure I can quite express what is so basic, so right, so utterly human about cooking and eating together.

—JOSHUA BECKER

Rosemary 76

By Pescado Rooftop Bar

Ingredients

- 1 ounce citrus vodka
- ½ ounce freshly squeezed lemon juice
- ½ ounce rosemary syrup
- Splash of Champagne or Cava
- Rosemary sprig, for garnish

Directions

Combine vodka, lemon juice, and rosemary syrup in a cocktail shaker. Add ice and shake. Strain into a chilled martini glass and top with Champagne or Cava. Garnish with a torched rosemary sprig, and enjoy!

An Après-Beach Hot Spot
Culinary Delights Abound *at* 30Avenue

When the real estate developers at Corr Group created 30Avenue, their mission was to provide Northwest Florida locals and visitors with an upscale indoor-outdoor destination for shopping, dining, entertainment, and office locations. The beautiful lifestyle center features stone-paved sidewalks, a central green for relaxing, multiple fountains throughout the property, majestic palm trees, and generous parking for its array of unique shops, restaurants, and businesses.

Cornerstones of the 30Avenue dining scene include Chef Tim Creehan's Cuvee 30A and Chef Tom Catherall's new Aja Elevated Asian Cuisine. Corchis Hospitality Group created a genius two-for-one dining experience in adjoining spaces on 30Avenue's east wing, where diners can grab margaritas and tacos at amigos 30A Mexican Kitchen or opt for homemade pasta, pizza, and more from amici 30A Italian Kitchen. What could be better? On the west end, breakfast is a way of life at Canopy Road Café, a classic American diner serving mouthwatering breakfast and lunch items daily.

Sprinkled between these are a handful of other experiences for dining, snacks, and retail. Southern Charm Coffee & Gather, founded by *Cupcake Wars* alumnus Jeff Martin, features freshly brewed coffee, desserts, pastries, sandwiches, and more. Goatfeathers has been a favorite along nearby Scenic Highway 30-A since 1988. Its beautiful 30Avenue location is a full-service seafood market and an excellent spot for dine-in or take-out meals, such as fresh shrimp, Gulf fish, oysters, crab legs, homemade soups, and more. Lastly, 30A Olive Oil Co. has all the handcrafted flavors of olive oil and balsamic vinegar you could ask for, plus cooking tools, dishware, home goods, spices, and gifts galore for the kitchen aficionado in your life.

Continually evolving and offering visitors events such as live music, festivals, holiday entertainment, and more, 30Avenue is a stop visitors should be sure to make on their next vacation and one that locals can rediscover time and again.

Chef Tim Creehan,
Cuvee 30A

Strawberry Basil Margarita

By amigos 30A Mexican Kitchen

ALWAYS ENJOY WITH FRIENDS, FAMILY, AND FULL BELLIES.

Ingredients

- 2 ounces strawberry-infused tequila
- 1 ounce freshly squeezed lime juice
- 1 ounce basil simple syrup
- ½ ounce Cointreau

FOR THE STRAWBERRY - INFUSED TEQUILA

- Milagro Silver Tequila, 750-milliliter bottle
- Fresh-cut strawberries

FOR THE BASIL SIMPLE SYRUP

- 1 cup water
- 1 cup cane sugar
- 4–6 sprigs fresh basil

Directions

FOR THE STRAWBERRY-INFUSED TEQUILA:

Cut up fresh strawberries and add them to the bottle of Milagro Silver Tequila. Let the fruit infuse into the spirit overnight.

FOR THE BASIL SIMPLE SYRUP:

Combine the water and sugar in a saucepan. Tear basil sprigs and leaves into the saucepan, place on medium-high heat, and bring to a boil. Once boiling, turn heat to low and let simmer for 15 minutes. Strain the basil out of the syrup. Allow to cool fully before bottling in an airtight glass bottle, jar, or other container.

FOR THE MARGARITA:

Add all ingredients to a cocktail shaker and shake until well combined. Pour into a chilled rocks glass, top with ice, and garnish with fresh strawberry slices. *¡Salud!*

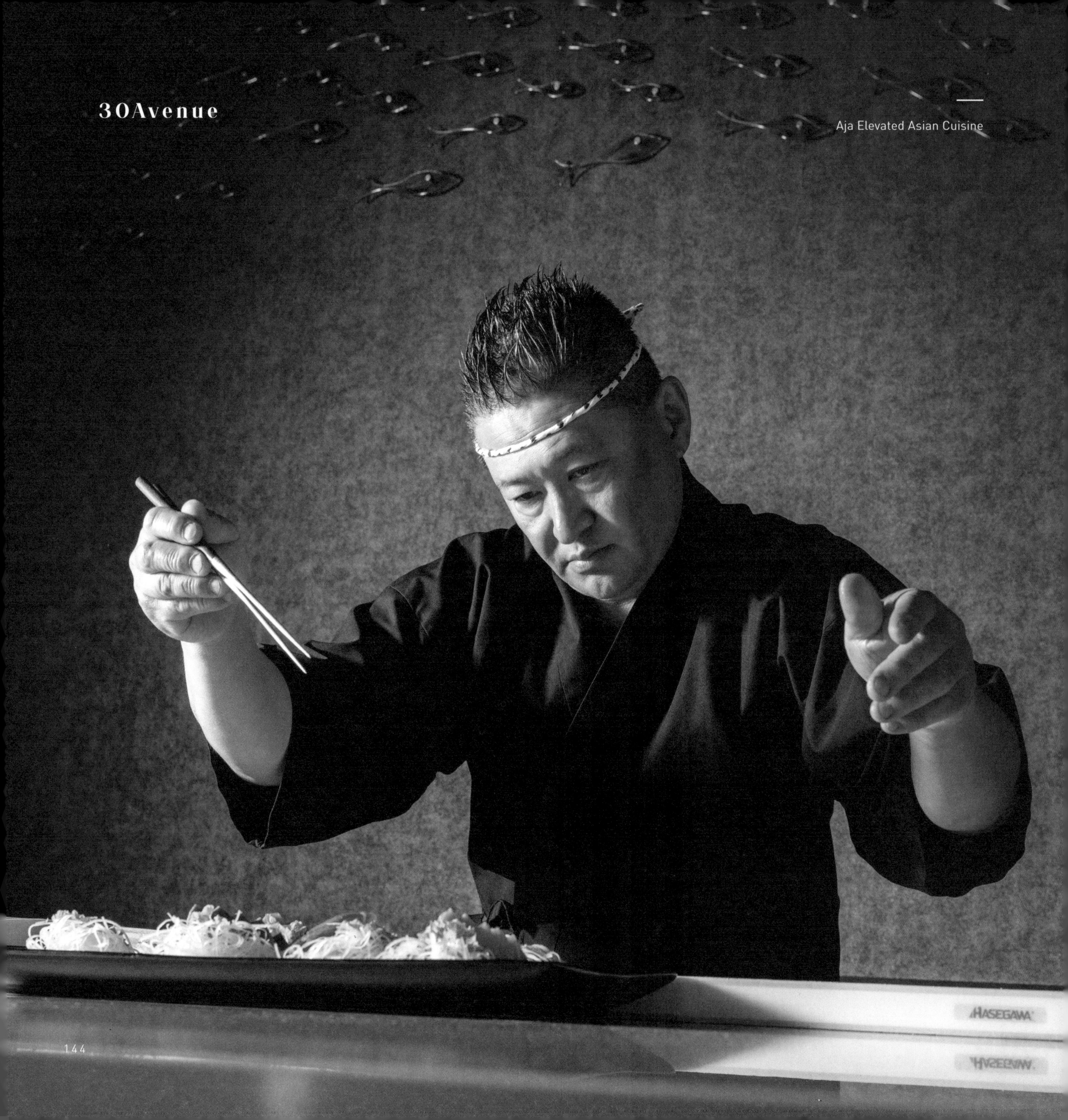
HASEGAWA

"

It's five o'clock somewhere.

—JIMMY BUFFETT

Panama City Beach & Beyond

We love PCB, where a laid-back Gulf of Mexico lifestyle meets fun and excitement for the whole family. From theme parks to state parks, Panama City Beach and its surrounding areas have no shortage of things to do and places to explore. The dining scene is no exception! Fresh seafood is king here, but award-winning cocktails, world cuisine, and food festivals are bountiful.

Serenity and Style
One Restaurant, Endless Experiences

Some restaurants simply lend themselves to special occasions: Valentine's Day, anniversaries, Thursday night . . . Any day is the perfect day for a visit to Firefly in Panama City Beach, Florida. From the moment you pass through the wooden front doors, you'll feel as if you've stepped into a cozy hideaway with an air of je ne sais quoi—it's difficult to pinpoint why, but you know you've found someplace special.

Firefly's owner, Dave Trepanier, attributes the success of his restaurant since it opened in 2007 to many things. "It's easy to say the food makes Firefly special, but it really is so much more than that," he says. "It's the whole experience—the service, the atmosphere, and the attention to detail."

Its motto is "casual fine dining," but Firefly boasts one of the most diverse menus in the area. With the addition of the sushi bar and multiple private dining rooms in 2013, the restaurant brought something for everyone to the table. Patrons can enjoy filet mignon and lobster in the main dining room underneath a beautiful, sprawling tree—complete with ambient lights and twinkling "fireflies" in its branches. "I wanted the warmth of a classic steakhouse with the intimacy of an outdoor Mediterranean bistro—that brought about the idea for the tree," Trepanier explains. "Then I thought about the fake fireflies in the tree, hence the name Firefly!"

The 535 Library Lounge is the perfect spot to cozy up with good friends, enjoy a drink while waiting for your table, or catch up on the week's events. The Firefly Bar has HD screens for watching the big game, and it's a great place for grabbing an appetizer or enjoying a full meal in a more casual setting. The sushi bar serves creative, delicious handmade rolls that are sure to impress. Combine all these elements with a robust menu that includes steaks, seafood, pasta, sushi, desserts, specialty cocktails, and over two hundred wines, and it's easy to see why Firefly has become a favorite dining destination for Panama City Beach locals and visitors alike.

Executive chef Rob Burgess took over the Firefly kitchen in 2019, adding some new dishes to the menu of staples that guests have loved since the restaurant opened in 2007. "My favorite thing about the Firefly menu is the variety of items," he says. "There are a lot of options without it being overwhelming to the customer—steaks, seafood, pasta, sushi. The abundance and availability of fresh local seafood are amazing, and the menu offers a mix of Southern-style food with a dash of Cajun-Creole influence and a little Italian flair."

Firefly has become a staple of fine dining in Panama City Beach, having hosted its share of celebrities: country music stars Jason Aldean and Toby Keith; professional athletes, including Heisman Trophy winners Pat Sullivan and Billy Sims and Baseball Hall of Fame great Bill Mazeroski; the legendary Tony Bennett; and even President Obama and the first family. Firefly is also the proud recipient of many accolades for fine dining, including OpenTable Diners' Choice Awards, Urbanspoon's list of America's Top 250 High-End Restaurants, *Wine Spectator*'s Award of Excellence, *Florida Trend*'s Golden Spoon Awards, and more.

Chef Rob Burgess

The Dark Horse

By Firefly PCB

Ingredients

- 2 ounces Horse Soldier Bourbon
- ¾ ounce lemon juice
- ¾ ounce simple syrup
- Handful of ripe blackberries

Directions

Muddle 2–3 blackberries and pour into a cocktail shaker with the liquid ingredients and fresh ice. Shake until the ingredients are well mixed, then strain over a large ice cube in a rocks glass. Garnish with a whole blackberry, and enjoy!

Saffron Arancini

By Firefly PCB

THIS ITALIAN STARTER IS A CROWD FAVORITE, WITH CRISPY RICE BALLS, THE PERFECT CHEESE BLEND, AND A CLASSIC RED SAUCE.

Ingredients

- 2 cups arborio rice
- ½ cup white wine
- 8 cups chicken stock, heated
- 1 onion, diced
- ¼ cup Parmigiano-Reggiano, grated
- ¼ cup fresh mozzarella, grated
- ¼ cup mascarpone cheese
- 1 tablespoon saffron
- 2 tablespoons olive oil
- Salt and pepper, to taste
- 2 cups herbed bread crumbs
- 1 cup flour
- 3 eggs, beaten
- 1 quart canola or vegetable oil
- Marinara sauce

Directions

In a large pot, heat olive oil. Sauté onion with saffron until soft. Add rice and coat with oil. Deglaze the pot with white wine.

Stir in hot chicken stock one ladle at a time, letting the stock absorb into the rice before adding any more. Once you have incorporated all the stock, finish with the three cheeses and stir well. Season with salt and pepper.

Cool the rice. Using your hands, roll it into one-ounce balls, then coat the balls in the flour, then the egg, then the breadcrumbs, shaking off any excess. Once thoroughly coated, set aside the rice balls and heat about four inches of canola or vegetable oil in a heavy-bottomed pot over medium heat.

Once the oil is around 375°F, place the rice balls in (be careful of popping oil!). You should do just a few at a time. Fry the arancini until golden brown around the outside and cooked throughout. Use a slotted spoon or spatula to remove the balls from the oil safely and set them on a paper towel–lined plate or tray while frying the remaining rice balls.

Place your cooked arancini on a serving dish or plate and top with grated Parmigiano-Reggiano and fresh herbs if desired. Serve with warm marinara as a topping or dip!

A Front Beach Road Icon

Thomas' Donut and Snack Shop in Panama City Beach, Florida, has been the area's doughnut specialist since 1971. Traditional glazed, cream-filled, iced, and countless flavored gourmet doughnuts are on offer, along with bear claws, crullers, fritters, and more. One stop at this walk-up roadside diner will make all your pastry dreams come true. Locally owned and operated since its inception, this charming dining destination has all the sweet treats you could hope for—including hand-dipped ice cream and milkshakes—as well as other American classics like burgers and sandwiches. Stop by and get a dozen doughnuts to go, or hang out on the deck and enjoy the gorgeous view of the Gulf of Mexico at this favorite among locals and visitors alike.

"

The best hour
of the day is
Happy Hour.

Events & Entertaining

Whether holding an intimate dinner party at home or hosting a lavish event for hundreds, you can find experts in all things entertainment along the beach communities of Northwest Florida. Designers, florists, caterers, mixologists, and planners converge in this beautiful corner of the world to share their expertise with locals and visitors alike.

Kelly Curry, Alexis Miller, Jordan Staggs, and Lisa Marie Burwell at Le Bon Ton, *VIE*'s Awards Party for Digital Graffiti Festival 2023 in Alys Beach

161

Passed Down to Be Passed Around

An ultrasmooth taste and family ties are the fuel that keeps Paul Sutton Bourbon growing strong. Produced in Danville, Kentucky, Paul Sutton Bourbon has been hailed as one of the best in its class since the inaugural bottled-in-bond, six-year-old, single barrel bourbon whiskey was released in 2021. Using local Alabama heirloom sweet corn and a sweet mash process instead of the usual sour mash, Paul Sutton Bourbon is distilled in a traditional eighteen-inch column still and meticulously aged in number-four-charred oak barrels to create a rich, hand-crafted product.

This Kentucky bourbon originated from an Alabama family legacy of seven generations. R.M. Sutton (the grandfather of Paul Sutton Bourbon founder Myra Barginear, MD)—along with his grandfather, father, and brothers—used to distill bourbon as a hobby when he wasn't taking care of his family, repairing shrimp boats, and training horses. Described as "pure goodness right from the get-go," Grandpa Sutton's exact mash recipe was unfortunately lost after he passed away—until Barginear and her husband, Paul Amrich, employed science to save it.

Barginear, a medical oncologist, revived her family's hundred-year-old mash recipe amid taking time off from her career to raise her children. She traded her lab coat for work boots and, in 2014, became the first woman cofounder and CEO of a family-owned and operated spirits distillery. Collaborating with an engineering firm, they used reverse engineering and analytical techniques to confirm the old family recipe contained in her grandfather's mason jars. Producing bourbon whiskey is a science and an art that requires innumerable resources and a great deal of patience. Barginear insisted on aging the bourbon for a minimum of six years to stay true to her family's traditions and quality bourbon—and for Barginear and her team, it was well worth it.

Paul Sutton Bourbon garnered numerous awards with its initial bottled-in-bond, six-year-old single barrel bourbon whiskey, including gold medals at the 2021 and 2022 World Spirits Competition, SIP Awards, ASCOT Awards, and John Barleycorn Awards. It can now be found on top shelves at a selection of handpicked bars and retailers, and each bottle is hand labeled, numbered, and dated. The words "Family Reserve" are embossed on the sides of the custom bottle to commemorate the family's hundred-year-old mash recipe, and seven vertical cuts on the back of the bottle represent seven generations of distilling. The bourbon's sweet finish, with notes of caramel, vanilla, citrus, and honey, make it an easy-sipping whiskey or a rich base for any Manhattan, whiskey sour, or bourbon smash.

163

Paul Sutton Bourbon

Many fans of Paul Sutton Bourbon prefer it neat or with an ice cube, but a favorite family cocktail recipe is the Paper Plane, with equal parts Paul Sutton Bourbon, Aperol, Amaro Nonino, and fresh lemon juice. The cocktail is a lovely balance of bitterness from the Aperol and brightness from the lemon juice. For the full effect, serve it in a coupe glass garnished with a small paper airplane. The 100-proof Paul Sutton Bourbon gives the drink a nice structure. The aforementioned bourbon smash is a perfect summer refresher: 2 ounces Paul Sutton Bourbon, 2 ounces seltzer, ½ ounce maple syrup, ½ ounce orange juice, ¼ ounce lemon juice, and 2 drops of Angostura bitters, served on the rocks and garnished with an orange slice.

Barginear and Amrich, both natives of southern Alabama, have strong ties to Florida's Emerald Coast. They have introduced their bourbon to the affluent whiskey and cocktail lovers in the area. Paul Sutton Bourbon has been the featured bourbon whiskey at several prominent local festivals and events, including 30A Wine Festival at Alys Beach, Taste of the Race in Seaside, VIE magazine's The Heritage – A VIE Legacy Show Home reveal party, and more. Cheers to family and great spirits!

"

Too much of anything is bad,
but too much good whiskey
is barely enough.

—MARK TWAIN

167

A Family Affair
From Foundation *to* Furnishings

A great kitchen is the heart of the home. It becomes the place where family and friends gather to eat and celebrate birthdays, engage in conversation, teach and learn new things, and just be themselves. It's a haven for healing and growing. The Owen Group, a boutique interior design firm based in Houston with a satellite office in WaterColor, Florida, knows that the key to creating and styling a beautiful kitchen lies in functionality and personality.

Founder and lead designer Tami Owen and her daughter, interior designer Brelan Owen Pearson, work with builders, architects, and homeowners from the earliest stages of a home's design. This ensures the finished space matches the vision of its residents and meets their individual needs.

The style of The Owen Group, which includes a handful of other talented designers and staff, could be described as classic elegance with a modern twist. Clean lines and contemporary art blend seamlessly with soft textures, elegant patterns, neutral palettes, and architectural details in each space the team designs. Sophistication, timeless style, and comfort are always top of mind, as Tami and Brelan focus on creating homey spaces that reflect the lifestyle and needs of each client.

On the following pages, you'll find examples of interiors by The Owen Group. One is a private home by Brickmoon Design architecture firm and built by Richard Price Custom Homes that features a gorgeous kitchen island and patterned backsplash. This home also has a stunning deep-blue wet bar area for entertaining or unwinding at the end of the day. Also shown is a contemporary gray kitchen in a Houston home designed by John Hathaway of Vanguard Studio and built by Art Duncan of Emerald Crest Development.

"We admire all aspects of design and appreciate different styles," say Tami and Brelan. "For us, it's about capturing our clients' individuality and taste."

Brelan Owen Pearson

Home by Brickmoon Design,
Richard Price Custom Homes, and
The Owen Group Interior Design

Home by Brickmoon Design,
Richard Price Custom Homes, and
The Owen Group Interior Design

Home by Brickmoon Design,
Richard Price Custom Homes, and
The Owen Group Interior Design

172

Home by John Hathway/Vanguard Studios, Art Duncan/Emerald Crest Developers, and The Owen Group Interior Design

Vegetable and hummus
tray by Shelly Harker,
A Life Styled

66

The key to a successful event is creating 'memory moments' by doing something unique and unexpected.

—SHELLY HARKER, *VIE* MAGAZINE

The Heart of the Home

Family gatherings, casual breakfasts, late-night chats, and birthday celebrations tend to happen in the heart of a home—the kitchen. Beautiful, thoughtful kitchen designs celebrate the fact that so much living takes place here, where good food and conversation nourish the body and soul. Melissa Skowlund, the founder and principal designer of Summer House Lifestyle in Grayton Beach, Florida, knows the importance of fashion *and* function in any space, and this gorgeous kitchen designed in partnership with Geoff Chick & Associates architecture firm and Chris Clark Construction is no exception.   .

Aptly named "Legasea," this stunning Gulf-front home exemplifies the sophisticated coastal style found along Scenic Highway 30-A. The design team kept this kitchen airy and bright by implementing a pecky cypress range hood, contemporary lighting, brushed gold accents, and a white-and-gray tile backsplash that stretches from counter to ceiling. The neutral palette is accented with metallic and navy, reflecting the beach, the golden Florida sun, and the shades of the shimmering Gulf just steps from the home. This is a kitchen worth celebrating!

The Joy of *Not* Cooking in Your Home

"I spent much of my time when I was younger with my grandmother in the kitchen and garden, where I learned the importance of paying attention to detail and maximizing every ingredient," says Chef Nathan Davis. In Bucksnort, Tennessee, where he grew up, he recalls, "I realized this was a place where food was a way of life. The produce has several seasons and various uses, from lettuces for a fresh salad to canning tomatoes for sauce during the winter. I mastered our family recipes and skills passed down from generation to generation and learned that creating a beautiful meal was always more meaningful when shared with family and friends."

At twenty-four years old, Davis's hard work and determination to become a great chef paid off, and he landed the sous chef position at a restaurant run by the Besh Restaurant Group in the Thompson Nashville hotel. He later moved from Nashville to the Gulf Coast of Northwest Florida, where he worked under famed chef Emeril Lagasse at Emeril's Coastal in Miramar Beach. This experience led to higher positions as chef de cuisine for Stinky's Fish Camp and award-winning Cuvée Kitchen + Wine Bar. Although he learned invaluable skills from all three restaurants, Davis wanted to be more personally involved in his patrons' dining experiences and spend more time at home with his daughter. This calling drove him to start his private chef service. "Through sharing my love for food and family, I designed the Polished Chef to help others create those moments that will last a lifetime."

Chef Nathan Davis

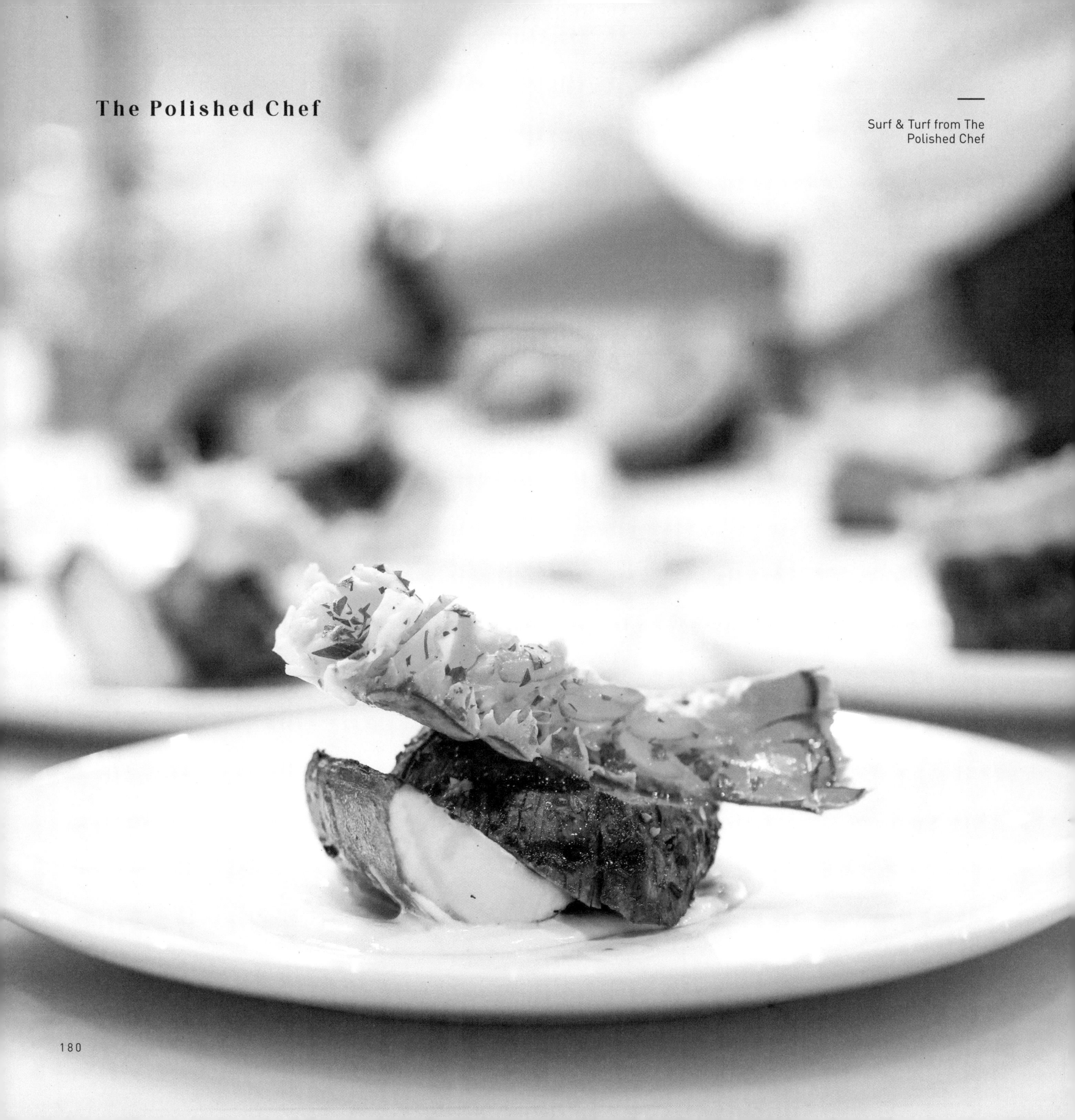

The Polished Chef

Surf & Turf from The Polished Chef

> "

I don't do things just for money or glamour; there has to be a heart and soul to it for me to say yes.

—CHEF EMERIL LAGASSE, *VIE SPEAKS* PODCAST

Emeril's Coastal,
designed by Geoff Chick
& Associates, Lovelace
Interiors, and Alden Lagasse

183

Life Is Better Together
Cheers *to the* Good Times

Beverage director and mixologist extraordinaire Christine Tarpey aims to combine flavor, flair, and friendship with her bar-on-the-go concept, Better Together Beverage. Founded along the Emerald Coast of the Florida Panhandle, her company provides unique cocktail-centric experiences, including mixology seminars, themed-event bars, custom beverage menus, and more.

Tarpey and her team will set up a custom bar at your event or special occasion and bring the fun while they do it. From dressing in tastefully themed outfits to providing glassware and accessories, the Better Together team creates one of the most memorable beverage experiences on the coast. Working with clients' needs and visions means no two events are alike, and the communities along Scenic Highway 30-A and beyond are big fans of this premiere beverage concierge.

Customized cocktail menus for weddings, parties, and showers are also available, and Tarpey has curated the bar menus for some of the area's best restaurants, including The Citizen in Alys Beach. Her love of craft cocktails is evident in her continually evolving offerings. She travels throughout the US for inspiration and educational experiences, from Napa Valley to New Orleans. She also works closely with local and regional purveyors of fine spirits, including Distillery 98 in Santa Rosa Beach, Florida, whose Dune Laker Vodka is filtered through oyster shells for an ultrasmooth taste.

Raising the bar for exciting parties and unique cocktails is the name of the game for Better Together Beverage. Whether taking artisan products and mixing them to craft a perfect libation or uniting loved ones to orchestrate memories that will last a lifetime, Tarpey says her goal is to "promote the idea that life is better together."

Mixologist Christine Tarpey

Love Letters

By Better Together Beverage

THIS IS A COCKTAIL FULL OF GRATIFICATION AND LOVE!

Ingredients

- 1 ounce vodka
- 1 ½ ounces pink lemonade
- ¼ ounce rose syrup
- ¼ ounce lemon juice
- Sparkling wine
- Dehydrated food-grade rose petals, for garnish
- 1 mini envelope
- 1 mini clothespin
- Coupe glass or martini glass

Directions

Place all ingredients except the sparkling wine in a cocktail shaker with ice and shake well. Strain into a coupe glass and top with sparkling wine.

Sprinkle in a pinch of dehydrated rose petals for garnish. Then, write your guest an uplifting message on the mini envelope and pin it to the rim of the glass. XOXO

Hibiscus Mai Tai

By Better Together Beverage

DON'T MISS OUT ON THIS ULTIMATE BEACH VACAY SIPPER.

Ingredients

- 1 ½ ounces silver rum
- 1 ounce fresh pineapple juice
- 2 ounces hibiscus-thyme tea concentrate (directions follow)
- ½ ounce crème de cassis
- ¼ ounce lemon juice
- 1 mint sprig, for garnish
- 1 honey dipper wand
- Collins glass or tiki glass
- 1 agave straw (optional)
- Ice, regular or pebble

FOR THE HIBISCUS-THYME TEA CONCENTRATE:
(Yields 4 Servings)

- 3 hibiscus tea bags
- 3 thyme sprigs
- 2 ounces bee pollen honey (or regular honey)
- 1 ½ cups water

Directions

FOR THE HIBISCUS-THYME TEA CONCENTRATE:

Boil water and measure out 1 cup. Add the tea bags and thyme to the hot water and let steep for 30 minutes. Strain and stir in honey until fully dissolved. This concentrate also makes a great "mocktail"—just add lemon soda water!

FOR THE COCKTAILS:

Shake all ingredients in a cocktail shaker over ice, pour ingredients into a collins glass, and add more ice to the top of the glass.

Garnish with a mint sprig and honey wand, and add an agave straw if you like. Cheers!

Pear Lychee
Martini from Bijoux

Designing for a Culinary Legend
An Architectural Vision

"I prefer my work to speak for itself," says architect Geoff Chick, based in the Florida Panhandle near the white-sand beaches of Scenic Highway 30-A. "Many people can talk a good game about architecture, but you know a great project when you see it." The Boston-born creative always enjoyed sketching and drafting, but it wasn't until he started seeing architecture as art that it clicked for him as a profession. Now he is one of the most highly sought-after architects for residential and commercial projects on Northwest Florida's Gulf Coast.

A kitchen is the heart of any home, and Chick's kitchen designs are a spectacular blend of form, function, and fashion. Hundreds of Gulf-front and beach-adjacent homes fill his portfolio, but perhaps one of his most unique projects is the interior build-out of Emeril's Coastal. The celebrity chef's casual fine-dining destination in Grand Boulevard Town Center at Sandestin is a shining example of understated elegance with an energetic vibe that befits iconic chef Emeril Lagasse perfectly.

Having lived in the area for decades, Emeril and his wife, Alden, wanted to open a restaurant along the Gulf Coast for a while before making the dream a reality in

Emeril's Coastal

This page and opposite:
Kitchen designs by Geoff
Chick & Associates

2017 with the opening of Emeril's Coastal Italian (now Emeril's Coastal). Its emphasis on fresh seafood and a deep connection to the local waters, farmers, and culture make it a perfect spot for enjoying the flavor of the area while getting the famous Emeril touch—a hint of New Orleans flair, Italian influence, and celebrity recognition, especially when the man himself is in the kitchen.

Alden Lagasse had a vision in mind for the restaurant's interiors. She worked closely with Geoff Chick & Associates on the design details and materials. The chef's counter, the central cocktail bar, and an expansive patio for casual outdoor seating around fire pits are vital features bringing guests the warm, inviting atmosphere they love. Susan Lovelace of Lovelace Interiors, who also happens to be Alden's cousin, worked in tandem with Chick and the Lagasses to bring the interior furnishings, artwork, and decor to fruition. The result is an ambience that complements the coastal menu using spectacular local art, nature-inspired textures, and modern touches.

Craft cocktail featuring
local Distillery 98 Dune
Laker Vodka, curated for a
private event by CC.Boone

"Promote the idea that life is better together.

—CHRISTINE TARPEY, *VIE* MAGAZINE

Curating Experiences
One-of-a-Kind Events *for* Any Occasion

No matter how much a couple, a family, or a group of friends loves going out for dinner, the experience can sometimes get stale. We fall into a rut, going to the same restaurants and ordering the same menu items. Even though they're delicious and we love the staff who have come to treat us like family, it's occasionally good to break out of our routine and try something new. That's where Caroline Boone comes in.

The owner and lead designer of CC.Boone Creative & Culinary Experiences in Santa Rosa Beach, Florida, specializes in "après beach" events. She and her team set up dreamy picnics, boho lounge decor, sumptuous charcuterie spreads, and entertainment for clients visiting the beach, locals celebrating special occasions, and businesses throwing soirees. Her casual elegance and breezy style perfectly suit those looking for an elevated picnic or outdoor lounge for bachelorette parties, girls' getaways, birthdays, and much more. CC.Boone can set up on the white-sand beaches, in a backyard, on a porch, or anywhere the vibes are right.

"Saltwater Supper Club was created as a way for us to create a charming dining experience right in the heart of your home," Boone says. She partnered with other locals who share her passion, reviving the art of the dinner series by curating events patrons could buy tickets to and hosting commissioned dinners for clients who want to invite their loved ones or celebrate a special occasion at home.

"Our team is small, and we like to take the time to get to know the people at the table," says Boone. "Maddie Bilderback, our culinary director, is such an easy presence and makes everyone feel right at home—literally. Bill Leavy is our head chef, and his approach to food is always very well thought out. His passion for cooking really shows up in his dishes, and he's the friendliest chef you'll ever meet!" Creating memorable meals with fresh Gulf seafood, local produce, and creative cocktail setups has been the foodie formula for many successful Saltwater Supper Club events throughout the past year.

Boone says good music, the right people, and candlelight can take your dinner party a long way. "Good quality, locally sourced food is also important. We also like to change it up by incorporating seasonal native foliage, block-print tablecloths, and curated playlists." Custom-printed menus, signature cocktails or mocktails, wine pairings, and grazing boards are also available to give each supper club event a one-of-a-kind feel.

Caroline Boone

A Guide to Charcuterie

By CC.Boone

Style Tip:

Begin with your cheeses and add a large filler, then finish your board with all additional food selections. Cheers!

1 HERB FOR GARNISH

- rosemary, thyme, oregano

1 LARGE FILLER

- whole pear, half pomegranate, whole apple, whole satsuma, whole orange, etc.

1 BUNCH OF GRAPES

- regular or cocktail

1 DRIED FRUIT

- apricots, pineapple, prunes, dates, citrus

1 RAW FRUIT

- figs, cherries, apples, assorted berries

1-2 SPREADS

- honey, jams, hummus, etc.

2 MEATS

- salami, prosciutto, pepperoni, etc.

2 DIPPERS

- crackers, cheese straws, veggies, pita, bread

3 CHEESES

- 1 hard, 1 soft, 1 semisoft

3 CRUNCHY ITEMS

- pickles, olives, pickled okra, nuts, wasabi peas

203

"

The world is your oyster.

Fresh bay oysters from a farm in Apalachicola, Florida

Celebrating a *VIE* Legacy Show Home

A labor of love over two years in the making, The Heritage – A *VIE* Legacy Show Home was truly a one-of-a-kind residence, presenting its future owners with boundless opportunities for making memories on the Gulf of Mexico. Located conveniently in the private enclave of Heritage Dunes, a gated beachside community in Seagrove Beach, Florida, this 4,871-square-foot master-piece debuted in 2022 as the first of nine custom houses to be developed in the neighborhood by Bella Mare Real Estate Holdings.

Principal architect Gerald Burwell of Burwell Associates, designer of The Heritage show home and the eight subsequent homes, describes the debut residence as "inclusive." Its inviting south-facing entry welcomes visitors with a beautiful plunge pool and surrounding courtyard, protected by a custom wooden screen and reminiscent of Southern gardens. The home was crafted with precision by the talented and steadfast team at Grand Bay Construction, and interior designer Duce May of Duce & Company seamlessly combined numerous design elements through-out, resulting in a dynamic space that is both unanticipated and pleasing to the eye.

Entertaining here is a breeze, with the airy, vaulted great room, ample deck and patio space, three immaculately designed wet bars, and an outdoor grill area. The home was put to the test during its exclusive grand reveal celebration, which featured celebrity chefs Emeril and E.J. Lagasse, preparing heavy hors d'oeuvres in the kitchen, and special guest Julian Lennon, whose spectacular fine-art photography was showcased throughout all four floors of the home.

We hope the story of this house is just the beginning of memories to be made in Heritage Dunes for years to come!

Chefs David Slater, Tommy Wachter, and Emeril Lagasse at The Heritage – A *VIE* Legacy Show Home in Seagrove Beach

Emeril Lagasse and Julian
Lennon at The Heritage
show home reveal party
in September 2022

Fresh honeycomb
and charcuterie by
Emeril's team

Everything is better

with sprinkles.

Life in Bloom

Celebrating the beauty, tenacity, and transformative nature of life itself, Metamorph Blooms offers floral arrangements that are more than just decorative gifts—each one is an experience. Founder and designer Allyson Justice Longshore started the project in 2020 in Santa Rosa Beach, Florida, when the COVID-19 pandemic uprooted her from working full-time in the fashion industry in New York City and inspired her to settle by the area's white-sand beaches where she had lived part-time. While Longshore still works with clients across the US, styling and building their wardrobes with exquisite designer pieces, her passion project is her boutique orchid business. Each Metamorph Blooms arrangement includes the chrysalis of a monarch butterfly lovingly attached to one of the stems.

Anyone who receives one of these gorgeous arrangements or purchases one for themselves is in for a treat a few days later as the butterfly emerges from its protective shell and takes flight. Those who wish to give this beautiful gift can order an orchid online for safe shipping or visit the Metamorph Blooms studio by appointment. Longshore says she hopes to introduce more floral and butterfly species in the future, but she is incredibly passionate about bringing awareness to the plight of the endangered monarch.

"My life feels much more aligned now than before the pandemic, and I owe a lot of that to the monarch butterfly and our beautiful beaches," Longshore shares. "The best part about this company is the hope it brings to humans and a species that desperately needs our help. It is very healing and gratifying work."

Allyson Justice Longshore

215

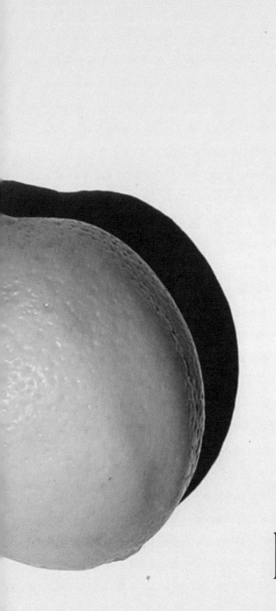

When life gives you lemons, grab the vodka and call your friends.

A Picnic Alfresco

Imagine walking onto a white-sand beach with the waves rolling gently in the background. An elegant yet undeniably bohemian table sits low in the sand, surrounded by comfortable cushions and throws, laden with printed cloths, flowers, and an array of fresh fruits, grazing boards, and light bites. Casually stunning picnics are the specialty of Tia Glenn, the owner and lead event designer at Fresco Picnic Co. based in Santa Rosa Beach, Florida.

"The beauty of the outdoors has always inspired us, and it is the perfect place to celebrate," Glenn says. She and her team at Fresco offer impeccably curated high-end picnic experiences that include seating and decor and expertly designed floral arrangements to make any occasion special. Add-on packages are also available for food and beverages, entertainment, photo backdrops, and more.

Any birthday, anniversary, proposal, bachelorette party, or company function will surely be memorable when you're dining and laughing with friends, surrounded by the beauty of nature and Fresco's exquisite designs. Glenn, who is from Birmingham, Alabama, also offers her services to clients in that area so that they can enjoy a Fresco picnic too!

Macarons from Firefly PCB
at the *VIE* Lawn Party, the
awards celebration for
the 2022 Digital Graffiti
Festival in Alys Beach

Shelly Harker

A Life Styled
Creating Monumental Moments

Planning a party or special event takes a lot of organization, imagination, and willpower. For those unsure of how to pull off an idea or who don't feel confident creating an event on their own, hiring an event designer can make all the difference between a fete and a flop. Shelly Harker, a Northwest Florida native and graduate of Florida State University's psychology program, has always been enchanted with art and photography. Still, it wasn't until after she gained her doctorate in clinical psychology, ran her own practice, and became a mom that she shifted her focus to the more creative career of event styling.

Harker was living in Atlanta when, as she puts it, running a private psychology practice alongside motherhood "put my life at a crossroads." She continues, "I closed the door to my practice and became reacquainted with my passion for art, design, and event planning—but from a unique vantage point, one informed by my years of training."

In 2022, she moved back to the beach community along Scenic Highway 30-A in Florida and started A Life Styled, a boutique event-planning company specializing in elegant, intimate events, themed parties, and corporate functions.

She explains, "Psychology is embedded in every facet of life, so having an in-depth knowledge of human behavior gives me a more intentional and intimate understanding of my clients and their needs. Together, we work to cultivate a distinct personal style that communicates something meaningful, something from within. Understanding human needs and motivation also helps to identify more captivating and authentic means of engagement, like tapping into the senses to create memorable moments."

A gorgeous fruit tray by
Shetly Harker,
A Life Styled

"

I drink to make other people more interesting.

—ERNEST HEMINGWAY

Index

Photo Credits

Salar Abduaziz/Miami Creative Agency, courtesy of The Daytrader: Pages 4, 26–27

Hannah Grace Abuvala, courtesy of Roux 30a: Pages 71, 73

Alissa Aryn Photography, courtesy of Black Bear Bread Co.: Page 79

Lauren Athalia: Pages 100, 205, 212, 213, 212, 215

Mary Grace Bethea, courtesy of CC.Boone: Page 201

Michael Booini, courtesy of Seagar's: Pages 39, 40, 43

Chloé Brennan, courtesy of Metamorph Blooms: Pages 213, 214

Hunter Burgtorf: Pages 16, 22–23, 37, 161, 206–207, 208, 209, 220–221

Claudia Casbarian with Julia Soefer, courtesy of The Owen Group: Page 173

Katie DeSantis: Pages 109, 110, 114–115, 123, 125, 126–127, 128, 129, 130–131, 187, 188

Wes Frazer, courtesy of Alys Beach: Page 103

Jack Gardner: Pages 176–177, 194, 195

Brittany Godbee, courtesy of A Life Styled: Page 174

Ed Gutentag, courtesy of Linda Miller Real Estate: Pages 8–9

Brenna Kneiss: Pages 54–55, 68, 75, 76, 89, 97,

Rachel Alyse Manning, courtesy of The Owen Group: Pages 169, 170–171, 172

Romona Robbins: Pages 6–7, 11, 29, 31, 32, 35, 47, 48–49, 51, 56–57, 59, 60–61, 62, 65, 66–67, 69, 81, 82, 85, 92–93, 104–105, 117, 118, 121, 136, 146–147, 151, 152, 190–191

Julia Kate Mace San Juan: Page 113

Kiana Tate Photography, courtesy of CC.Boone: Pages 196, 199, 202–203

Collis Thompson, courtesy of Pescado: Page 135

Dawn Chapman Whitty: Page 149

Gaby Yerden: Front cover

Courtesy of 30Avenue: Pages 141, 142, 144, 145

Courtesy of A Life Styled: Pages 222–223, 224–225

Courtesy of Alys Beach: Page 99

Courtesy of Better Together Beverage: Page 185

Courtesy of Bud & Alley's: Pages 90, 95

Courtesy of Emeril's: Pages 13, 14, 15, 17, 18, 21, 183, 192, 193

Courtesy of Firefly PCB: Page 155

Courtesy of Fresco Picnic Co.: Pages 218–219

Courtesy of Paul Sutton Bourbon: Pages 163, 164–165, 167

Courtesy of Pescado: Page 139

Courtesy of The Citizen: Pages 107, 108

Courtesy of The Pearl Hotel: Page 133

Courtesy of The Polished Chef: Pages 178–179, 180, 181

Courtesy of Visit Panama City Beach: Pages 156–157